SELECTION OF AUTHENTIC RECIPES

THE ORIGINAL
GREEK
COOKING

FOTORAMA

SELECTION OF AUTHENTIC RECIPES

THE ORIGINAL
GREEK
COOKING

RECIPES
ALEXANDROS VALAVANIS

PHOTOGRAPHY
YIORGOS DEPOLLAS

FOOD PREPARATION AND STYLING
TASSOS TOLIS

TRANSLATION
MARIA ANTONIOU

INTRODUCTORY TEXT
DIMITRIS KOROVESSIS

FOTORAMA

Published and produced in Greece
by editions FOTORAMA
52,Sina str. 106 72 Athens.
Tel: (01)3643592 Fax: (01)3643323
Publishing Manager: Alexandros Valavanis
Photography: Yiorgos Depollas
Photography Assistant:Dimitris Pazaitis
Food Preparation and Styling: Tassos Tolis
Design and Art Direction:
Dimitris Korovessis - Tina Danon

Colour reproductions: A.Bastas D.Plessas
Montage: Petros Kapellas
Printing: Chaidemenos S.A.

Many thanks to the Federation of Greek
Wine Industries for the information and
the photographs on Greek wines.

VARIETY OF GREEK CHEESES (page 6)
BANK OF THE EVINOS RIVER IN ETOLOACARNANIA (right)
VARIETY OF APPETIZERS. UNDER THE SHADOW OF THE.
VOLCANO OF SANTORINI (THERA) (page 10-11)

OWNER OF A TAVERN IN A VILLAGE OF MYCONOS ISLAND

CONTENTS

PUBLISHER'S PREFACE

GASTRONOMY: The science of art of choosing and preparing food.

Have you ever wondered what the exact meaning of one of the most popular words is and where it comes from? Gastronomy ... A word deriving from Greek which shows the exact attitude to life of a people.

More than 150 recipes specially selected from different regions of Greece reveal the secrets of the authentic Greek cuisine. The most important elements of an everlasting tradition in one book. A guided tour into the wonderful world of Greek food. A world which without the olive oil, without the "kakavia" and the "mageiritsa", without the "feta" cheese, would never represent the heart of real Greece.

THE ORIGINAL GREEK COOKING contains more than 90 colour photographs, which graphically convey the beauty and the sensitivity of the people and the country. A country which has put its seal on this distinctive quality of culinary expression through the diversity of the countryside.

The recipes have been carefully selected and tested and specially photographed for this book. We truly believe that it will help you to approach the rich tradition of the Greek cuisine.

FISH SOUP (BOUILLABAISSE) WITH BACKDROP
THE ISLAND OF PAROS (left, recipe page 44)

15

A TAVERN IN PELOPONNESE

WORK OF THE FOLK PAINTER THEOFILOS FROM LESVOS ISLAND

INTRODUCTION TO GREEK CUISINE

"Life's fundamental principle is the satisfaction of the needs and wants of the stomach. All the important and trivial matters depend on this principle and cannot be differentiated from it."

Epicurus
Hedonist philosopher

If you should ever (God willing...) be invited to an authentic Greek table you would have great difficulty overcoming the surprise brought about from the bombardment of diffused sensations and tastes. It would be equally difficult for you to find explanations and justifications for these sensations in cook books. Greek cuisine guards its secrets well from those who would seek to strip away its mysteries...

Its savourings spring forth unforeseen and spontaneous, casting a spell over the mys-

17

RIVER IN KARPENISSI (page 18-19)

tics of its myth who will see it as a descendant of the ancient Greeks and a true born child of nature which gave birth to them.

Greece is a sea faring country with charming mountain ranges and small fertile plains. The smell of the sea blends with the smell of oregano and thyme from the mountains. The bright sun bewitches the colours and the breeze, at times cool and refreshing, at other times wild and angry, bursts forth to welcome the "change", the moving force of this small land. The scenery constantly changes and it is only through these changes that the restless soul of the Greeks finds rest.

These people created one of the brightest civilizations ever to be seen thousands of years ago. An offspring of this civilization was the idea of "good living" whose gastronomical facet led taste to its greatest glories. The Romans continued this tradition, preserving the palatial treasures which they took from the Greeks and glorified them in their famous feasts. The element of excess, which was and still is foreign to the Greek temperament,was eliminated by the later Byzantines, thus preserving the authenticity of Greek cuisine for over a thousand years. The Turks who realised Byzantium had for years previously been affected by its cuisine since they had grown up under Byzantine influence.

Contemporary Greek cuisine has wrongly been considered a mixture of Turkish and Italian cuisines since it is found in the roots of all Mediterranean tastes. Many of the modern recipes have remained unchanged for over twenty centuries retaining the original savouring shades since the basic ingredient of all the recipes is the famous Greek olive oil,which is distinct from all others in the Mediterranean. Here is how Aristophanes, in the Frogs, describes a feast which was prepared in honour of Hercules: "...As soon as Persephone heard that you had arrived she kneaded bread, she set three cauldrons of fava on the fire and over the burning embers she roasted an entire ox, as well there were pies and many sweets". The exaggeration of the Aristophanean words reveal the exact opposite in terms of excess. Only as a theatrical finding could it be useful for in reality the "fertile and rich but low yielding earth", as the ancient Greek writers characterised Greek soil, gives everything sparingly but never lacking in quality or variety. "The ideal is not abundance" generalised Socrates,a dinner guest at the most famous feast in the world who revealed the opinion the Greeks had towards food: the satisfaction of all the senses, the pleasure of both the body and the soul.

Even today the contemporary Greek knows that what makes a perfect feast is above all good company. Food is prepared in accordance to the tastes of the dinner guests whether spicy, light or heavy, roasted or fried and always accompanied by a carefully chosen wine which allows for the role of the "comuner". The dinner conver-

sation always centres around the food but it is conducted in such a manner as to be affable and to create the appropriate gastronomical atmosphere. The host will draw attention to the well cooked lamb and potatoes pointing out that the lamb was brought from a certain village (not any one in particular but one which was chosen by the host) and how the salad, which is aglow from the olive oil, is the best in quality because it is local and of his own choice and preparation. Thus the person who will attempt to cook Greek food must bear in mind that aside from the particular manner of cooking and the local dishes, the cuisine has a great deal of pride, hospitality, enthusiasm and nobleness as well as a great deal of personal opinion which is a representative detail of its creations. It is a common secret that the Greeks view the olive, the bread and the wine as symbols of life. They are never absent from the home and they are never thrown out. This is another basic tenant of the cuisine which surrounds these products. The olive, the fruit of the sacred tree, is processed in many ways. Oiled or vinegared, crushed or flavoured with oregano, shrivelled or cut, they accompany practically all dishes. The most well known are the olives of Kalamata which can be found prepackaged all over Europe. This fact, however, by no means diminishes the value or quality of the other olive types.

The oil, as noted above, transgresses the entire history of Greek cuisine allowing for the continuity of taste throughout the centuries.Moreover, Greek oil is deemed to be the best in the world by culinery experts

while nutritionists consider it a requisite supplement for all diets crediting it with therapudic properties. The Greeks will never give it up or exchange it and they often hold long and heated debates as to which region produces the best oil.

Bread (as well as rusk, preferably Cretan) is the requisite accompaniment to all meals. Often bread served with feta cheese or rusk served with tomato and olives make for a wonderful snack or even a quick and simple meal while in the country.

The wine which is the third element of the basic ones that make up Greek cuisine has been known for thousands of years. It is praised in the Homeric epics and its birth is associated with a variety of Dionysian myths. Satyrs, tipsy from wine, perform the first circular dance in Attica. On another occasion once again indulging in wine and abandonment of the Dionysian ecstasy, they deliver the first theatrical oration ever to be heard in the world. It is justifiable then that wine should have a place of honour at a Greek table and indeed it often is the reason for inviting people to dinner.

When two friends meet a common phrase heard is:"...We must get together and drink something" this phrase serving as the invitation to dinner. Although they say "drink" they do not mean "becoming drunk" but rather to become gladdened since aside from good food, wine is what gladdens the heart, loosens the tongue and

brings people closer. At feasts, the ancient Greeks often chose as wine bearer the one who was strongest, that is the one who could withstand the wine. It was his responsibility to oversee and determine the amount of water to be mixed with the wine to maintain the guests relaxed and in good humour so that the conversation could flow more smoothly. It seems that contemporary Greeks continue this tradition offering wine at their invitation while continuing to drink after the meal. Apart from the traditional retsina, white wines made of pink grape are preferred and which are made locally in Kefalonia and the Mainland as well as in the Cyclades and on Crete. They are served chilled and accompany seafood dishes or appetizers. The Mediterranean musk flavoured red wine does not lack in followers as well as the more delicate tasting wines made from a variety of European grapes. In the last few years Greek wine is slowly gaining recognition since an ever growing number of brave local vineyards are bottling their own.

A fact which may surprise French connoisseurs of cheese is that Greece holds the first place for cheese consumption per person in all of Europe. Thus in accordance with the good mood, feta which has been known for centuries, accompanies the traditional country salad but can also be an appetizer, which accompanies ouzo, served with oil, oregano and pepper or served

plain or used as a full ingredient in one of the many Greek pies. The spicy Kefalotiri made from goats milk is a product of the islands. As well, the different types of gruyere made from a mixture of cow's and goat's milk supplement a meal and often augment the flavour of the dishes they accompany.

The famous Greek yoghurt, creamy and sourish is freely used as a basic ingredient for the famous tzaziki which can accompany any meal. It can also be topped with honey and walnuts and served as the perfect culmination to a rich meal preluding to, as the song says, more amorous inclinations. It is well known that the passionate feelings the Greeks have are characterised by a roughness which they have never been ashamed of. On the contrary, this characteristic has infiltrated into their cuisine as atested by the number of recipes whose basic ingredients are aphrodisiacs.

We could go on at some length describing the different products and their place at the Greek table. But even the revelation of each product's mystery becomes monotonous in the end, simply because the mystery of a Greek meal is you yourself who will enjoy it and who will once again attempt to find these paths of taste and savour which are lost in the depths of the centuries.

Therefore we recommend that you organise your own "ouzo ritual" with a variety of appetizers. Do away with the individual plates and share the various appetizers with friends! Your appetizers must make an impression with their different savouring tastes and never served in quanity. Pour ouzo into the glasses and let time stand still. Avoid over-indulging in the food and let the ouzo slowly speak for itself. The body should not be directed towards the table since the purpose of an "ouzo ritual" is the play with the different tastes and flavours-never satiety. A little fun, a little teasing, letting the eye wander about the surroundings and absolutely no solemnity...This is the prologue to a Greek table without any boundaries.

If you should ever find yourselves in the beautiful countryside or on the magical islands of Greece, seek out the good food. Leave the centre and walk through the narrow lanes and the out of the way neighbourhoods. There, in a small courtyard under a traditional vine bower you may

discover, if you are lucky, small temples dedicated to taste. And if the cook should-look at you a trifle too intently while you are eating, don't be bothered! A smile is a praise of their good cooking ability and it's what they are expecting. A Greek, you see,is a theatrical figure who always seeks an audience and applause.

Today, where European cuisines shine surrounded by gold cutlery and stylish maitres, gastronomical pleasure is lost amid complicated etiquette procedures and formalities. In Greek cuisine you will rediscover the original feeling of taste. If ac-

companied by a mouthwatering preparation, then it can certainly lead you to that peak of sensuality which was first referred to at the beginning of this heading.

For the end we have saved a wonderful recipe for fried fish which is recommended by fishermen and which we feel is the best way to begin your experience of Greek cuisine. Fry the fresh fish in a pan of heated olive oil. Place onto the plates while still hot and crunchy. Enjoy them with a chilled Greek white wine and...

...To your health!

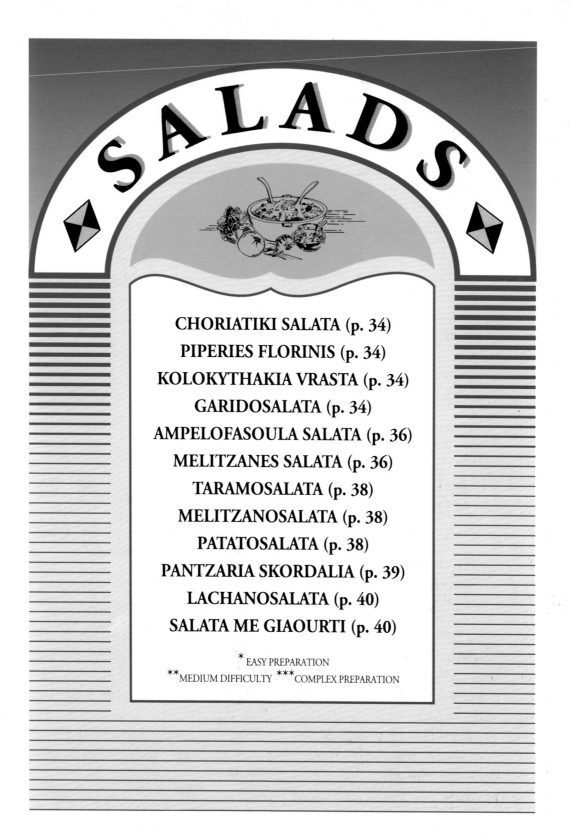

SALADS

*EASY PREPARATION
**MEDIUM DIFFICULTY ***COMPLEX PREPARATION

AN OLD LADY IN FOLEGANDROS ISLAND

Arkadia

CHORIATIKI SALATA   *

GREEK COUNTRY SALAD

- ◆ 1 kilo TOMATOES UNRIPE
- ◆ 1 MODERATE SIZED ONION
- ◆ 1 GREEN PEPPER, 1 CUCUMBER
- ◆ 80 gr. OLIVES
- ◆ 180 gr. FETA CHEESE
- ◆ DRIED OREGANO
- ◆ 80 gr. OLIVE OIL
- ◆ VINEGAR, SALT

Slice the tomatoes and the cucumber, arrange on a plate, season with salt and add the onion and the green pepper cut in rings. Add dried oregano, the feta cheese and pour the olive oil and some vinegar over them.

FOR 4 PERSONS

Macedonia

PIPERIES FLORINIS   **

PEPPERS FROM FLORINA

- ◆ 1 1/2 kilo RED PEPPERS FROM FLORINA
- ◆ 2 - 5 CLOVES GARLIC
- ◆ 1/2 CUP PARSLEY FINELY CHOPPED
- ◆ OIL, VINEGAR, SALT

Wash the peppers and bake in a pre-heated oven at 250° C. When the skin turns black on both sides, take them out and when cold, clean them removing the skin and the seeds.
Place the peppers on a plate, add the garlic, the parsley and the oil-vinegar sauce and season with salt.

FOR 8 PERSONS   *Photograph page 41*

Macedonia

KOLOKYTHAKIA VRASTA   *

COOKED COURGETTES

- ◆ 1 kilo SMALL COURGETTES
- ◆ FRESH MINT FINELY CHOPPED
- ◆ 1/2 TEACUP OLIVE OIL
- ◆ 3 TABLESPOONS VINEGAR
- ◆ SALT

Put the courgettes in a saucepan with water to cover and add salt to taste. Cook until there is no water left, add the vinegar and the mint. Season with salt. Cook for 3 - 4 minutes and turn the heat off. When cold, sprinkle with the olive oil and serve.

FOR 4 PERSONS   *Photograph page 37*

Attica

GARIDOSALATA   *

SHRIMP SALAD

- ◆ 1 LETTUCE FINELY CHOPPED
- ◆ 500 gr. MEDIUM SIZED SHRIMPS
- ◆ 2 BOILED EGGS SLICED
- ◆ 1 GREEN PEPPER SLICED
- ◆ 3 TABLESPOONS OLIVE OIL
- ◆ 2 TABLESPOONS VINEGAR
- ◆ PARSLEY AND FENNEL FINELY CHOPPED
- ◆ SALT

Cook the shrimps in salted water with a little vinegar for 10 minutes. Clean and arrange them on a plate along with the lettuce, the eggs, the parsley, the fennel and the pepper. Beat the oil with the rest of the vinegar and pour the mixture over the salad.

FOR 4 PERSONS   *Photograph page 38*

Corfu

AMPELOFASOULA SALATA   *

SALAD WITH STRING BEANS

- ◆ 1 kilo STRING BEANS CLEANED
- ◆ 150 gr.OLIVES
- ◆ 2 TOMATOES SLICED
- ◆ 1/2 TEACUP OLIVE OIL
- ◆ 3 TABLESPOONS VINEGAR ◆ SALT

Put the spring beans in a saucepan with plenty of water and some salt and cook for 10 minutes uncovered so as not to lose their colour. Drain and let them dry. Place them in a salad bowl along with the tomatoes and the olives. Season with salt. Beat the olive oil with the vinegar seperately and pour the sauce over the salad.

FOR 6 PERSONS

Attica

MELITZANES SALATA   **

SALAD WITH AUBERGINES

- ◆ 2 MEDIUM SIZED AUBERGINES
- ◆ 1 ONION FINELY CHOPPED
- ◆ 2 TOMATOES SLICED
- ◆ 1 GREEN PEPPER SLICED
- ◆ 1 CUCUMBER SLICED
- ◆ 2 TABLESPOONS CHIVES
- ◆ 1/2 TEACUP OLIVE OIL ◆ SOME OLIVES
- ◆ SALT ◆ DRIED OREGANO

Bake the aubergines in a moderate oven for 40 minutes. When cold, peel them and cut in pieces. Place them in a salad bowl and mix with the remaining ingredients.

FOR 4 PERSONS

SALAD WITH AUBERGINES (top left)
COOKED COURGETTES (bottom left)
SALAD WITH STRING BEANS (right)

Macedonia

SALATA ME GIAOURTI   *

SALAD WITH YOGHOURT

- ◆ 2 TOMATOES ◆ 1 CUCUMBER SLICED
- ◆ 400 gr. POTATOES SLICED
- ◆ 1 SMALL LETTUCE FINELY CHOPPED
- ◆ 1 EGGYOLK, 2 EGGS BOILED
- ◆ 1 DESSERTSPOON HOT MUSTARD
- ◆ 3 TABLESPOONS OLIVE OIL
- ◆ SALT ◆ 1 TABLESPOON SUGAR
- ◆ 1/2 kilo YOGHOURT STRAINED

Wash and cook the potatoes and cut in cubes. Place them in a salad bowl and add the lettuce, the tomatoes, the eggs (cut in four) and the cucumber. Mix well and season to taste with salt.

Beat the yoghourt, the eggyolk, the mustard, the oil, the sugar and some salt until smooth.

Pour the sauce over the salad.

FOR 6 PERSONS

Kefalonia

LACHANOSALATA

WHITE CABBAGE SALAD

- ◆ 1 SMALL WHITE CABBAGE
- ◆ 1 LEMON (JUICE), 3 CLOVES GARLIC
- ◆ 5 DESSERTSPOONS OLIVE OIL
- ◆ 1 CARROT ◆ SALT

Wash the cabbage and the carrot and chop them finely. Place in a salad bowl. Pound the garlic in a mortar. Season with salt and add the lemon juice. Pour the sauce over the cabbage, add the olive oil and serve.

FOR 6 PERSONS

SOUPS

* EASY PREPARATION

**MEDIUM DIFFICULTY ***COMPLEX PREPARATION

TAVERN IN CHANIA, CRETE

Epirus

MAGEIRITSA   ***

SOUP ON EASTER NIGHT (ENTRAILS AND HERB)

- ◆ LAMB ENTRAILS
- ◆ SOME LAMB INTESTINES
- ◆ 300 gr. SPRING ONIONS FINELY CHOPPED
- ◆ 1/2 CUP OLIVE OIL
- ◆ THE INNER LEAVES OF 1 LETTUCE FINELY CHOPPED
- ◆ 1/2 TEACUP PARSLEY FINELY CHOPPED
- ◆ 1/2 TEACUP DILL FINELY CHOPPED
- ◆ 1 TABLESPOON FLOUR
- ◆ 1 TEACUP WHITE WINE
- ◆ 6 TABLESPOONS RICE
- ◆ 3 EGG YOLKS
- ◆ JUICE OF 2 LEMONS
- ◆ SALT ◆ PEPPER

Wash the entrails and put them for a few minutes in hot water and then in cold. Drain and cut into small pieces. Wash the intestines, rub with lemon and salt, rinse in water. Scald in hot water, drain and cut in small pieces.

Heat the olive oil in a saucepan and brown the onions and the lettuce and add the flour, the dill, the parsley, the wine, the entrails with the intestines, salt and pepper to taste and 5 glasses of water. Cook over a moderate heat for almost 30 minutes and add the rice. Cook for 20 minutes and turn the heat off.

Beat the eggyolks adding slowly the lemon juice and then some stock from the pot. Stir in the mixture into the saucepan. Serve hot.

FOR 6 - 8 PERSONS

Cyclades

KAKAVIA   ***

FISH SOUP (BOUILLABAISSE)

- ◆ 1 kilo FISH FOR SOUP
- ◆ 1/2 kilo SMALL ROCK FISH
- ◆ 1/2 kilo SHRIMPS
- ◆ 1 SMALL LOBSTER
- ◆ 2 ONIONS
- ◆ 2 POTATOES
- ◆ 4 CARROTS
- ◆ 4 COURGETTES
- ◆ 3 TOMATOES
- ◆ 1 CUP OLIVE OIL
- ◆ 1 STALK CELERY WITH LEAVES
- ◆ 1 LEMON (JUICE)
- ◆ SALT ◆ PEPPER

Clean the fish and pour the lemon juice over them. Put the vegetables in boiling water and let until half-cooked. Add the fish, salt to taste and cook over a moderate heat for 15 minutes.

Take the big fish, the shrimps, some carrots, courgettes and celery to garnish the fish. Cook the rest until mashed. Put into a strainer and squash to take all the pulp. Clean the lobster, cut it into pieces and put it with the pulp and the oil in the saucepan and cook for some minutes. Turn the heat off.

Place the big fish on a plate, garnish with the vegetables and season to taste with salt and pepper.

Serve the soup seperately with fried bread.

FOR 6 - 8 PERSONS   *Photograph page 14*

SOUP ON EASTER NIGHT WITH BACKDROP THE VILLAGE PAPIGGO, EPIRUS

APPETIZERS-PIES

* EASY PREPARATION
**MEDIUM DIFFICULTY ***COMPLEX PREPARATION

Macedonia

AVGA ME NTOMATA KAI FETA   *

SCRAMBLED EGGS WITH TOMATO AND FETA CHEESE

- ◆ 1/2 kilo TOMATOES
- ◆ 4 EGGS
- ◆ 200 gr. FETA CHEESE CRUMBLED
- ◆ 1 HOT PEPPER
- ◆ 100 gr.FRYING OIL
- ◆ SALT ◆ PEPPER

Peel and grate the tomatoes. Heat the oil in a frying pan. Put the tomatoes in the pan and cook until there is no water left.
Beat the eggs and add the feta cheese and the pepper. Season with salt and pepper. Stir well. Turn the heat down and simmer until the eggs are ready.

FOR 4 PERSONS

Crete

AVGA ME MELITZANES TIGANITES   **

EGGS WITH FRIED AUBERGINES

- ◆ 3 AUBERGINES
- ◆ 6 EGGS
- ◆ 1 TEACUP FRYING OIL
- ◆ RED PEPPER ◆ SALT

Slice the aubergines in rings 2 cm thick each, season with salt and leave them for 1 hour. Rinse and dry.
Heat the oil in a frying pan and add the aubergines. When one side is fried, turn them over. Put an egg on each aubergine ring.Season with salt and pepper.
Fry until the yolk of the egg is ready.

FOR 6 PERSONS

Chios

OMELETA KOLOKYTHAKIA   *

OMELETTE WITH COURGETTES

- ◆ 1 kilo SMALL COURGETTES
- ◆ 6 EGGS
- ◆ 1 TEACUP FETA CHEESE COARSELY CHOPPED
- ◆ SALT, PEPPER
- ◆ FRYING OIL

Wash the courgettes and put them in salted water. Strain and slice them. Put them in a bowl and add the cheese.
Heat the oil in a frying pan. Beat the eggs and pour them in the pan. Turn the heat down. Place the courgettes over the eggs. Turn the omelette on the other side. Fry the omelette over a low heat until it is ready.

FOR 4 PERSONS

Thessaly

MANOURI TIGANITO   *

FRIED MANOURI CHEESE (WHITE UNSALTED CHEESE)

- ◆ 500 gr. MANOURI CHEESE
- ◆ 1 EGG
- ◆ 1 TEACUP FLOUR ◆ FRYING OIL

Cut the manouri cheese in a triangle shape. Beat the egg and dip the manouri cheese first in flour and then in the egg. Heat the oil in a frying pan and fry it. Serve hot.

FOR 4 PERSONS

SCRAMBLED EGGS WITH TOMATO AND FETA CHEESE (centre right)
EGGS WITH FRIED AUBERGINES (bottom right)
OMELETTE WITH COURGETTES (top)
FRIED MANOURI CHEESE (bottom left)

Epirus

SPANAKOPITTA   ***

SPINACH PIE

- ◆ 1 kilo SPINACH COARSELY CHOPPED
- ◆ 500 gr. LEEKS FINELY CHOPPED
- ◆ 300 gr. FETA CHEESE CRUMBLED
- ◆ 1 ONION FINELY CHOPPED
- ◆ DILL ◆ FRESH MINT
- ◆ 2 EGGS ◆ 1 TEACUP OIL

FOR THE PASTRY SHEETS
- ◆ 1/2 kilo FLOUR
- ◆ 1 TEACUP WATER ◆ 1 TEACUP OIL
- ◆ SALT ◆ PEPPER

Wash the spinach and parboil it. Strain well.

Heat the oil in a saucepan and fry the onion and the leeks until golden brown. Turn the heat off and add the spinach, the feta cheese and the eggs beaten.

Season with salt, pepper, fresh mint and dill. Mix well.

Put the flour, the water, the oil and salt in a bowl. Knead well. Divide the dough in ten balls and leave them for 1 hour covered. Flatten each ball with a thin rolling pin on a floured pastry board and roll out to a thick pastry sheet.

Oil a baking pan and place five pastry sheets in it brushing each one with oil. Spread the spinach filling evenly. Cover with five more pastry sheets brushing each one with oil. Cut the pie with a sharp knife from one end of the pan to the other.

Bake in a pre-heated oven at 200° C for 40-50 minutes.

FOR 8 - 10 PERSONS

Roumeli

KOLOKYTHOPITA   ***

COURGETTE PIE

- ◆ 2 kilos BIG COURGETTES ◆ 2 ONIONS
- ◆ 1 TEACUP OIL ◆ 1/2 GLASS MILK
- ◆ 1 TABLESPOON BUTTER
- ◆ SALT ◆PEPPER
- ◆ 1/2 kilo FETA CHEESE CRUMBLED
- ◆ 5 EGGS ◆ DILL

FOR THE PASTRY SHEETS
- ◆ 1 kilo FLOUR ◆ 300 gr. YOGHOURT
- ◆ 2 EGGS
- ◆ 1 TEACUP OIL

Wash and grate the courgettes.

Heat the oil and the butter in a saucepan and fry the onions until golden brown. Strain the courgettes well and put them in the saucepan. Season with salt and pepper. Cook until there is no water left. Turn the heat off. Add the feta cheese and the eggs beaten. Season with dill.

Mix well.Put the yoghourt and the oil in a bowl. Mix well. Add the eggs stirring continuously. Add the flour and water if necessary. Divide the dough in ten balls and leave covered for 1 hour. Flatten each ball with a thin rolling pin on a floured pastry board and roll out ten thick pastry sheets.

Oil a baking pan and place five pastry sheets brushing each one with oil.

Spread the filling evenly. Cover with five more pastry sheets brushing each one with oil.

Bake in a pre-heated oven at 250° C for an hour.

FOR 8 PERSONS

SPINACH PIE (left) COURGETTE PIE (right)
CHEESE PIE (bottom) CHEESE PIES WITH SESAME (top)

FISH-SEAFOOD

* EASY PREPARATION
**MEDIUM DIFFICULTY ***COMPLEX PREPARATION

A FISHERMAN IN GYTHIO - PELOPONNESE

Macedonia

GARIDES SAGANAKI   *

BAKED SHRIMPS WITH CHEESE

- ◆ 6 MEDIUM SIZED SHRIMPS
- ◆ 3 SMALL TOMATOES PEELED
- ◆ 1/2 TEASPOON OUZO
- ◆ 1/2 HOT PEPPER
- ◆ 2 TABLESPOONS OLIVE OIL
- ◆ 50 gr. FETA CHEESE
- ◆ SALT, SOME SUGAR

Wash the shrimps and put in an earthenware or fireproof dish. Add all the ingredients except the feta cheese. Bake at 200° C for 20 minutes. Add the feta cheese 5 minutes before turning the heat off.

FOR 1 PERSON

Macedonia

MYDIA PILAFI   **

MUSSELS WITH RICE

- ◆ 1 kilo MUSSELS
- ◆ 2 TEACUPS RICE
- ◆ 1 ONION FINELY CHOPPED
- ◆ 1 TEACUP OLIVE OIL
- ◆ 3 TOMATOES FINELY CHOPPED
  WITHOUT THE SEEDS
- ◆ 1 TEACUP WHITE WINE
- ◆ SALT ◆ PEPPER

Clean the mussels and wash thoroughly.
Put the olive oil, the onion and the mussels in a saucepan and fry until the onion is golden and the mussels open. Add the wine and the tomatoes. Season with salt, pepper and cover with hot water.
Cook over a low heat for 15 minutes.
When the water left is almost 4 teacups

(add if necessary), add the rice. Cook until there is no water left.
Serve with the shell or without.

FOR 6 PERSONS

Attica

KSIFIAS SOUVLAKI   **

SWORD FISH SOUVLAKI

- ◆ 1 kilo SWORDFISH
- ◆ 4 TOMATOES NOT RIPE
- ◆ 4 GREEN PEPPERS
- ◆ 1 TEACUP OLIVE OIL
- ◆ 2 LEMONS (JUICE)
- ◆ OREGANO ◆ SALT

Cut the fish, the tomatoes, the green peppers and the onions in cubes of the same size. Place the cubes on the skewers. Season with salt and oregano.
Bake in a very low oven until done.
Serve with the lemon juice and the oil whisked in a different bowl.

FOR 4 - 6 PERSONS   *Photograph page 77*

Samos

MARIDAKI TIGANITO ME KREMMYDIA **

FRIED WHITEBAIT WITH ONIONS

- ◆ 1/2 kilo SMALL WITEBAIT
- ◆ 2 kilos ONIONS SLICED
- ◆ COARSE SALT ◆ FLOUR
- ◆ FRYING OIL

Wash the fish, strain and season with salt. Mix the fish with the onions and the flour. Heat the oil in a frying pan and fry the fish on both sides.
Strain and serve hot.

FOR 6 PERSONS   *Photograph page 57*

BAKED SHRIMPS WITH CHEESE (bottom)
MUSSELS WITH RICE (top)

Kefalonia

GAVROS FOURNOU ★★

BAKED ANCHOVY

- ◆ 1 kilo ANCHOVY
- ◆ 1/2 kilo RIPE TOMATOES FINELY CHOPPED
- ◆ 1 TEACUP PARSLEY FINELY CHOPPED
- ◆ 6 CLOVES GARLIC
- ◆ 1 TEACUP OLIVE OIL
- ◆ SALT, PEPPER

Clean the anchovy removing the heads and the intestines. Wash thoroughly. Arrange in an oiled baking pan with all the ingredients except the parsley. Bake in a very hot oven for 10 minutes and then turn the heat down at 150° C and cook for 30 more minutes. Serve garnished with the parsley.

FOR 6 PERSONS

Kefalonia

BAKALIAROS SCORDALIA ★★★

FRIED COD WITH GARLIC SAUCE

- ◆ 1 kilo DRIED COD
- ◆ 500 gr. MILK
- ◆ 500 gr. FRYING OIL
- ◆ 1 TEACUP GRATED TOAST

FOR GARLIC SAUCE SEE APPETIZERS, PAGE.61.

Slice the cod and put in water for 12 hours. Change water 2-3 times. Drain. Arrange the slices on a plate with the skin upwards. Pour the milk over it and let until it is absorbed. Dip the slices in the grated toast and fry in hot oil.
Serve with garlic sauce.

FOR 4-6 PERSONS

Spetses

PSARI A LA SPETSIOTA ★★

BAKED FISH "A LA SPETSAE"

- ◆ 1 FISH WEIGHING 1-1 1/2 kilo (GROUPER, SEA-BREAM)
- ◆ 1 TEACUP OLIVE OIL
- ◆ 500 gr. FRESH TOMATOES SLICED
- ◆ 1 TEACUP WHITE WINE
- ◆ 1/2-1 TEACUP PARSLEY AND DILL FINELY CHOPPED
- ◆ 2 CLOVES OF GARLIC FINELY CHOPPED
- ◆ 250 gr. ONIONS SLICED
- ◆ 1 TABLESPOON TOMATO PUREE
- ◆ 1 LEMON
- ◆ SALT ◆ PEPPER

Wash and clean the fish. Slice and sprinkle with salt.
Put in an oiled baking pan and cover with the onions. Sprinkle with the wine. Beat the olive oil with the tomato puree, salt and pepper. Pour over the fish. Add the parsley, the garlic with the dill, and the tomato. Bake in a moderate oven for 30 minutes.
Serve garnished with lemon slices and fresh parsley.

FOR 6 PERSONS   *Photograph page 72*

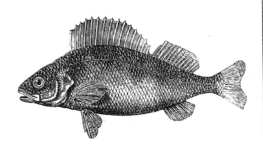

71

FRIED COD WITH GARLIC SAUCE (left)
BAKED ANCHOVY (right)

BAKED FISH "A LA SPETSAE"

Cyclades

BARBOUNIA MARINATA ***

RED MALLET MARINATED

- ◆ 8 BIG RED MALLETS
- ◆ 8 CLOVES OF GARLIC FINELY CHOPPED
- ◆ SOME ROSEMARY
- ◆ 1 kilo TOMATOES
- ◆ 3 TABLESPOONS VINEGAR
- ◆ 1 TABLESPOON FLOUR
- ◆ 1/2 TABLESPOON SUGAR
- ◆ SALT, PEPPER
- ◆ FRYING OIL
- ◆ FLOUR FOR BATTER

Remove the scales and the intestines and wash the red mallets. Drain and sprinkle with salt. Dip the red mallets into the flour and fry in a frying pan. Drain.

Strain the oil into a bowl and pour back in the pan adding the flour. Strain the tomatoes and put the juice in the pan. Add the vinegar, the garlic and season with rosemary, salt and pepper. Cook sauce until it thickens. A few minutes before it is completely set, add the sugar. Finally, add the red mallets.

Serve garnished with finely chopped parsley.

FOR 4-6 PERSONS

RED MALLET MARINATED (bottom)
BAKED GROUPER WITH WINE (top)

MEAT - MINCED MEAT

*EASY PREPARATION
**MEDIUM DIFFICULTY ***COMPLEX PREPARATION

A SHEPHERD IN GALAXIDI

Patra

ARNI GIOUVETSI   **

BAKED LAMB WITH PASTA

- ◆ 1 kilo LAMB
- ◆ 1/2 kilo BARLEY-SHAPED PASTA or ANY OTHER KIND OF PASTA
- ◆ 5-6 RIPE TOMATOES FINELY CHOPPED
- ◆ 1 MEDIUM SIZED ONION FINELY CHOPPED
- ◆ 1 GARLIC FINELY CHOPPED
- ◆ 1 TEACUP OLIVE OIL
- ◆ 200 gr. GRATED CHEESE
- ◆ SALT ◆ PEPPER

Wash the meat and cut into serving pieces. Place in a baking pan. Add the tomatoes, the onion, the garlic, the oil and a glass of water. Season with salt and pepper.

Bake in a pre-heated oven at 280° C for almost 2 hours until brown. Turn the meat over and add 3 glasses of hot water. When the water starts boiling, add the pasta. Cook until there is no water left.

Sprinkle with cheese after removing it from the oven.

FOR 4 PERSONS

Roumeli

ARNI ME PRASA   **

LAMB WITH LEEK

- ◆ LEG OF LAMB WEIGHING 1.5 kilo
- ◆ 3-4 SPRING ONIONS FINELY CHOPPED
- ◆ 1 kilo LEEKS COARSELY CHOPPED
- ◆ 2 LEMONS (JUICE), 1 EGG
- ◆ 1 TABLESPOON FLOUR
- ◆ SALT ◆ PEPPER ◆ BAY LEAF
- ◆ 180 gr. OLIVE OIL

Heat the oil in a saucepan and brown. the onions. Cut the meat into serving pieces and put in the saucepan. Add salt, pepper, bay leaf, half the lemon juice, some water. Cook over a moderate heat for 40 minutes. Place the leeks in one side and cook over a low heat for 40 more minutes.

Beat the egg with the rest of the lemon juice and the flour adding some stock. Pour over the meat, stirring well. Turn the heat off.

Serve with fried potatoes.

FOR 6 PERSONS

Roumeli

ARNI EKSOHIKO   **

LAMB STUFFED WITH CHEESE AND POTATOES

- ◆ 1 LEG OF LAMB WEIGHING 1.5 kilos
- ◆ 2 ONIONS FINELY CHOPPED
- ◆ 180 gr. OLIVE OIL
- ◆ 3 POTATOES CUT IN CUBES
- ◆ 200 gr. CHEESE
- ◆ 1 TABLESPOON BUTTER
- ◆ 2 CLOVES OF GARLIC FINELY CHOPPED
- ◆ SALT, PEPPER

Wash the meat and cook in salted water for almost 1 hour. Remove the bone. Heat the oil in a frying pan and fry the onions and the garlic until golden brown. Add the potatoes and the cheese until golden brown. Turn the heat off.

Season the meat with salt and pepper and butter it. Stuff with the mixture.

Fold in aluminum foil not too tightly. Bake in a hot oven for almost 1 hour.

FOR 6 PERSONS

BAKED LAMB WITH PASTA (top) LAMB WITH LEEK (centre)
LAMB STUFFED WITH CHEESE AND POTATOES (bottom)

Chios

MOSCHARI ME ELIES   ✳✳
VEAL WITH OLIVES

- ◆ 1 kilo VEAL
- ◆ 250 gr. BIG GREEN OLIVES
- ◆ 500 gr. FRESH TOMATOES FINELY CHOPPED
- ◆ 180 gr. OLIVE OIL
- ◆ 2 BAY LEAVES
- ◆ SALT ◆ PEPPER

Cut the meat in serving pieces. Brown in hot oil on all sides. Add a glass of water and cook over a moderate heat for almost 2 hours or until tender. Add the tomatoes. When there is almost no water left, add the olives and the bay leaves. Season with salt and pepper. Cook for 5 more minutes and turn the heat off.
Serve with fried potatoes.

FOR 4 PERSONS

Macedonia

MOSCHARI ME DAMASKINA   ✳✳
VEAL WITH PRUNES

- ◆ 1 kilo VEAL
- ◆ 750 gr. PRUNES
- ◆ 2 ONIONS FINELY CHOPPED
- ◆ 2 BAY LEAVES
- ◆ 1/2 DESSERTSPOON CINNAMON
- ◆ 1/2 DESSERTSPOON SUGAR
- ◆ 1/2 kilo TOMATOES
- ◆ 180 gr. OLIVE OIL
- ◆ SALT ◆ PEPPER

Cut the meat in serving pieces.
Heat the oil in a saucepan and brown the meat on all sides. Add the onions and fry until golden brown. Pour the wine over it and add the tomatoes finely chopped and strained, the bay leaves, the cinnamon, the sugar. Season with salt and pepper. Cover with water. Cook over a low heat until the meat is tender. Place on a plate. Place the prunes on the bottom of the saucepan, add the meat and some hot water. Cook for 10-15 minutes.
Serve with rice.

FOR 6 PERSONS

Roumeli

MOSCHARI STIFADO   ✳✳
VEAL WITH ONIONS

- ◆ 1 1/2 kilo VEAL
- ◆ 1 1/2 kilo VERY SMALL ONIONS
- ◆ 1 GARLIC FINELY CHOPPED
- ◆ 180 gr. OLIVE OIL
- ◆ 2 TABLESPOONS VINEGAR
- ◆ 1 TABLESPOON TOMATO PUREE
- ◆ CINNAMON, CLOVE, OREGANO
- ◆ SALT ◆ PEPPER ◆ PIMENTO

Cut the meat in serving pieces.
Heat the oil in a saucepan and brown the meat on all sides. Clean the onions in lukewarm water. Add the onions, the garlic, the vinegar in the saucepan. Dissolve the tomato puree in 1/2 glass of water and pour over the meat. Season with the spices. Cook over a moderate heat for almost 2 hours adding lukewarm water if necessary.

FOR 6 - 8 PERSONS

VEAL WITH OLIVES (bottom) VEAL WITH PRUNES (right)
VEAL WITH ONIONS (top)

Macedonia

MOSCHARI ME KASTANA   ***

VEAL WITH CHESTNUTS

- ◆ 1 1/2 kilo VEAL
- ◆ 500 gr. CHESTNUTS
- ◆ 1 TEACUP WHITE WINE
- ◆ 2 ONIONS ◆ 5 CARROTS
- ◆ 300 gr. POTATOES
- ◆ 200 gr. CAULIFLOUR
- ◆ 1 SPRIG OF CELERY
- ◆ 200 gr. OLIVE OIL
- ◆ SALT ◆ PEPPER

Tie the meat with string.
Heat the oil in a saucepan and fry the meat on all sides until golden brown. Pour the wine over and add the celery, the carrots and the onions. Season with salt and pepper. Cover with water. Cook over a moderate heat for 2 hours. Clean the chestnuts and put them in the saucepan 30 minutes before turning the heat off. Add the potatoes and the cauliflour. When ready, slice the meat and put it on a plate. Remove the vegetables and the chestnuts from the saucepan and garnish the meat with them.
Stir in white wine and some flour (if necessary) to set the sauce. Pour it over the meat.

FOR 6 PERSONS

Corfu

SOFRITO   **

VEAL WITH GARLIC SAUCE

- ◆ 6 SLICES VEAL 2cm THICK
- ◆ 1/2 - 1 TEACUP PARSLEY FINELY CHOPPED
- ◆ 6 CLOVES OF GARLIC FINELY CHOPPED
- ◆ 1 TEACUP WHITE WINE

- ◆ 3 BAY LEAVES
- ◆ 180 gr. OLIVE OIL
- ◆ FLOUR
- ◆ SALT ◆ PEPPER

Cover the meat with flour and fry slightly. Strain the oil and add the garlic, the parsley and the bay leaves. Season with salt and pepper. Brown and pour the wine over them. Place in a saucepan, cover with hot water and cook over a moderate heat until tender.
Serve with mashed potatoes.

FOR 6 PERSONS

Peloponnese

MOSCHARI ME KOLOKYTHAKIA **

VEAL WITH COURGETTES

- ◆ 1 1/2 kilo VEAL
- ◆ 1 kilo COURGETTES
- ◆ 2 ONIONS FINELY CHOPPED
- ◆ 2 - 3 TOMATOES, PEELED AND FINELY CHOPPED
- ◆ 200 gr. OLIVE OIL
- ◆ SALT ◆ PEPPER ◆ FRESH MINT

Cut the meat into pieces.
Heat the oil in a saucepan and fry the onion until golden brown. Add the meat and fry on all sides. Add the tomatoes. Season with salt, pepper and fresh mint. Add 1/2 glass of hot water. Cook over a low heat for 2 hours.
Clean and chop the courgettes. Fry them slightly. Place them in one side of the saucepan. Cook over a very low heat for 10 minutes and turn the heat off.

FOR 6 PERSONS

VEAL WITH CHESTNUTS (top right)
VEAL WITH COURGETTES (left)
VEAL WITH GARLIC SAUCE (bottom)

Macedonia

VODINO ME LAHANO ***

BEEF WITH CABBAGE

- 1 1/2 kilo BEEF WITH BONE
- 1 kilo CABBAGE
- 1 LEMON (JUICE)
- 4 POTATOES ◆ 4 CARROTS ◆ 3 ONIONS
- 3 BEETS ◆ 5 TOMATOES (JUICE)
- 200 gr. YOGHOURT
- 180 gr. OLIVE OIL
- 4 SPRING ONIONS FINELY CHOPPED
- 3 SPRIGS OF CELERY FINELY CHOPPED
- 1/2-1 TEACUP PARSLEY FINELYCHOPPED
- 1/2-1 TEACUP DILL FINELY CHOPPED
- 1/2 TEACUP BUTTER
- 5 BAY LEAVES
- 2 GREEN PEPPERS SLICED
- 2 RED PEPPERS SLICED
- COARSE BLACK PEPPER ◆ SALT

Cut the meat in pieces and cook for 20 minutes. As it begins to boil remove scum which is formed on top. Add one onion, two potatoes, two carrots, the bay leaves and season with coarse black pepper.

Cook over a high heat for 1 hour.

Remove the vegetables and add the two onions, the beets cut in cubes and the cabbage finely chopped. Saute the spring onions in the butter. Put them in the saucepan. Add the rest of the carrots and the potatoes cut in cubes, the peppers, the parsley, the celery and the dill. Cook for 1 hour.

Mash the vegetables that have been removed and add them in the saucepan together with the lemon juice, the tomato juice and the oil and cook for 15 minutes.

Place a tablespoon of yoghourt on each plate before serving.

FOR 6 - 8 PERSONS

Macedonia

SYKOTAKIA ME PIPERIES *

LAMBS' OR CALVES' LIVER WITH PEPPERS

- 500 gr. LAMBS' OR CALVES' LIVER
- 500 gr. GREEN PEPPERS
- 500 gr. RIPE TOMATOES
- 1/2-1 TEACUP PARSLEY FINELY CHOPPED
- 1 TEACUP OLIVE OIL
- SALT ◆ PEPPER

Peel and chop the tomatoes finely. Slice the peppers removing the seeds. Put the oil in a saucepan and add the tomatoes, the peppers and the parsley. Cook until the tomato juice is absorbed. Cut the liver in small pieces. Put them in the saucepan and simmer for almost 1 hour.

FOR 6 PERSONS

Volos

SPETZOFAI **

VILLAGE SAUSAGES AND PEPPERS CASSEROLE

- 1 kilo VILLAGE SAUSAGES
- 2 RED PEPPERS FINELY CHOPPED
- 2 GREEN PEPPERS FINELY CHOPPED
- 2 ONIONS SLICED ◆ 100 gr. OLIVE OIL
- 1 TOMATO FINELY CHOPPED

Heat the oil in a saucepan. Fry the onions until soft. Add the sausages cut in small pieces, the peppers and the tomato. Cook over a moderate heat for 15 minutes. Serve hot.

FOR 6 PERSONS

BEEF WITH CABBAGE (top)
LAMBS' OR CALVES' LIVER WITH PEPPERS (left)
VILLAGE SAUSAGES AND PEPPERS CASSEROLE (right)

Euboea

GIOUVARLAKIA AVGOLEMONO ✶✶
MEATBALLS WITH EGG AND LEMON SAUCE

- ◆ 1 kilo MINCED MEAT (BEEF OR VEAL)
- ◆ 2 TEACUPS RICE
- ◆ 2 EGGS
- ◆ 1 ONION FINELY CHOPPED
- ◆ 1 TEACUP PARSLEY FINELY CHOPPED
- ◆ 1 TEACUP OLIVE OIL
- ◆ 1 TEACUP DILL FINELY CHOPPED
- ◆ SALT ◆ PEPPER
- ◆ 2 EGGS
- ◆ 2 LEMONS (JUICE)

Mix the minced meat with the onion, the parsley, the rice, half the oil, salt and pepper and the two eggs. Shape small meatballs - the size of a walnut - and arrange on a plate covered with the dill. Put the rest of the olive oil in a saucepan, add the meatballs and cook over a low heat for 1 hour. When there is no water left, add another glass of water and bring to the boiling point.

Beat the whites of the two eggs with a fork. Add the yolks and the lemon juice slowly beating continuously. Add some stock from the saucepan and pour the egg and lemon sauce over the meatballs.

FOR 8 PERSONS	*Photograph page 99*

Chios

MOUSSAKAS ✶✶✶
BAKED AUBERGINES, POTATOES, MINCED MEAT WITH CREAM

- ◆ 1/2 kilo MINCED MEAT (BEEF OR VEAL)
- ◆ 750 gr. POTATOES SLICED
- ◆ 750 gr. BIG AUBERGINES SLICED
- ◆ 3 EGGS
- ◆ 500 gr. FRESH MILK
- ◆ 200 gr. GRATED CHEESE
- ◆ 1 ONION
- ◆ 1 STICK CINNAMON
- ◆ 500 gr. TOMATOES, PEELED
- ◆ 1/2 GLASS OLIVE OIL
- ◆ 100 gr. BUTTER
- ◆ 4 TABLESPOONS SEMOLINA
- ◆ SALT ◆ PEPPER

Fry the aubergines and the potatoes slightly. Brown the onion in a saucepan with the oil and add the tomatoes mashed without the seeds and the cinnamon. Season with salt and pepper. Stir well and turn the heat off.

Heat the butter in a different saucepan, add the semolina and brown. Beat the eggs with the milk and pour in the saucepan. When set, turn the heat off. Add half the cheese.

Arrange a layer of potatoes in an oiled baking pan. Sprinkle with cheese. Cover with a layer of aubergines, sprinkle with cheese, then a layer with all the minced veal, sprinkle with cheese, a layer of potatoes, sprinkle with cheese and a layer of aubergines. Pour the cream over it and sprinkle with cheese.

Bake in a moderate oven for 40 minutes.

FOR 6-8 PERSONS	*Photograph page 103*

Smyrna

SOUTZOYKAKIA SMYRNEIKA ✶✶
SMYRNA SAUSAGES

- ◆ 700 gr. MINCED MEAT (BEEF OR VEAL)
- ◆ 2 EGGS
- ◆ 2 SLICES OF BREAD
- ◆ 1/2 - 1 TEACUP PARSLEY FINELY CHOPPED

- ◆ 6 CLOVES OF GARLIC POUNDED
- ◆ 1 ONION FINELY CHOPPED
- ◆ 1 TABLESPOON VINEGAR
- ◆ 1 kilo TOMATOES PEELED
- ◆ 150 gr. OLIVE OIL
- ◆ 1 GLASS RED WINE
- ◆ 1/2 DESSERTSPOON SUGAR
- ◆ 200 gr. FLOUR
- ◆ FRYING OIL
- ◆ 1/2 DESERTSPOON CUMIN
- ◆ SALT ◆ PEPPER

Soak the bread and then strain. Put in a bowl and mix with the minced meat, the eggs, the garlic, the onion, the parsley, the cumin, the vinegar. Season with salt and pepper. Shape into sausage like rolls the size of a big cork. Dip into flour and fry slightly until brown. Strain.

To prepare the sauce: Heat 1/2 a cup of the olive oil in a frying pan, add 2 tablespoons flour, the wine, the tomatoes and the sugar. Stir continuously until the sauce thickens.

Place the sausages in a saucepan, pour the sauce over them and cook for 5 minutes.

Serve hot with rice.

FOR 6-8 PERSONS	*Photograph page 103*

Crete

AGINARES GEMISTES ***

ARTICHOKES WITH MINCED MEAT AND CREAM

- ◆ 10 ARTICHOKES
- ◆ 2 LEMONS
- ◆ 1/2 kilo MINCED MEAT (BEEF OR VEAL)
- ◆ 1 ONION
- ◆ 3 TABLESPOONS OLIVE OIL
- ◆ 1/2 GLASS OF WHITE WINE

- ◆ 4 TOMATOES
- ◆ 1 BAY LEAF
- ◆ 2 CLOVES
- ◆ SALT ◆ PEPPER

FOR THE SAUCE
- ◆ 4 TABLESPOONS FLOUR
- ◆ 4 TABLESPOONS BUTTER
- ◆ 500 gr. MILK
- ◆ 2 EGGS
- ◆ 1 TEACUP GRATED CHEESE
- ◆ 1 NUTMEG
- ◆ SALT ◆ PEPPER

Remove outer leaves and the inside of the artichokes with a spoon. Rub with lemon and salted water. Cook for 15 minutes and cut in half.

Heat the oil in a saucepan and fry the onion until golden brown. Add the minced meat stirring for 10 minutes and pour the wine over it. Strain the tomatoes and add the juice in the saucepan, the bay leaf, the cloves. Season with salt and pepper. Cook over a low heat until there is no water left. Stuff the artichokes with the mixture.

To prepare the sauce: Heat the milk, the flour and the butter in a small saucepan until the sauce thickens. Add the eggs beaten, the nutmeg, half of the grated cheese. Season with salt and pepper. Mix well and pour the sauce over the top of the artichokes. Place the artichokes in an oiled baking pan and sprinkle with the rest of the cheese. Add some water and bake at 180° C for almost an hour or until the cream is golden brown.

FOR 6 PERSONS	*Photograph page 105*

Crete

MELITZANES PAPOUTSAKIA   ***

BAKED AUBERGINES WITH MINCED MEAT AND CREAM

- ◆ 4 BIG AUBERGINES
- ◆ 400 gr. MINCED MEAT (BEEF OR VEAL)
- ◆ 1 ONION FINELY CHOPPED
- ◆ 1/2 TEACUP OLIVE OIL
- ◆ 2 RIPE TOMATOES FINELY CHOPPED
- ◆ 1/2 TEACUP PARSLEY FINELY CHOPPED
- ◆ SALT ◆ PEPPER
- ◆ FRYING OIL
- ◆ 1 TEACUP GRATED CHEESE
- ◆ 250 gr. FRESH MILK
- ◆ 1 EGG
- ◆ 1 TABLESPOON BUTTER
- ◆ 2 TABLESPOONS FLOUR

Cut the aubergines lengthwise so as to remove some of the inside. Sprinkle with salt and let them stand in water for an hour to draw the bitter juices.

Heat oil in a large frying pan and fry them slightly. Put fresh oil and heat it to brown the onion. Add the minced meat and stir for 5 minutes. Add the tomatoes without the seeds, the parsley and 1/2 glass of water. Season with salt and pepper. Cook over a moderate heat until there is no water left. Stuff the aubergines with the mixture (2 tablespoons for each aubergine) and arrange them in an oiled baking pan.

To make the sauce: Brown the flour slightly with the butter adding lukewarm milk slowly and stirring with a wooden laden. Turn the heat off when the sauce thickens. Beat the eggs, add salt and stir them in. Pour the sauce over the aubergines, sprinkle with the grated cheese. Add 1/2 glass of water in the baking pan. Bake in a

moderate oven until the sauce gets golden brown.

FOR 6 PERSONS   *Photograph page 105*

Patra

PASTITSIO   **

BAKED SPAGHETTI WITH MINCED MEAT

- ◆ 1/2 kilo SPAGHETTI No 5
- ◆ 1/2 kilo MINCED MEAT (BEEF OR VEAL)
- ◆ 1 1/2 TEACUP OLIVE OIL
- ◆ 2 TEACUPS GRATED CHEESE
- ◆ 1 TEACUP WHITE WINE
- ◆ 1 TABLESPOON TOMATO PUREE
- ◆ 2 CLOVES OF GARLIC FINELY CHOPPED
- ◆ CINNAMON ◆ SALT ◆ PEPPER
- ◆ 2 EGGS
- ◆ 5 TABLESPOONS FLOUR

Cook the spaghetti in boiling salted water. Drain before they are completely cooked. Return to the saucepan, add some oil mixing well. Add one teacup of grated cheese.

Heat some oil in another saucepan and brown the minced meat with salt and pepper, the garlic, the cinnamon and the tomato puree for 15 minutes.

To make the sauce: Put the milk with the flour and some salt in a saucepan over a low heat. Stir continuously until the sauce thickens.

Place a layer of spaghetti in a baking pan. Cover with the minced meat and then add a layer of spaghetti. Pour over the sauce, add some oil and the rest of the grated cheese. Bake in a moderate oven for 30 minutes.

FOR 8 PERSONS

BAKED SPAGHETI WITH MINCED MEAT (top)
MOUSSAKAS (left)   SMYRNA SAUSAGES (right)

Cyclades

TOMATES GEMISTES   **

STUFFED TOMATOES

- ◆ 8 BIG TOMATOES
- ◆ 350 gr. MINCED MEAT (BEEF OR VEAL)
- ◆ 2 ONIONS FINELY CHOPPED
- ◆ 180 gr. OLIVE OIL
- ◆ 1 GLASS OF WHITE WINE
- ◆ 1 BAY LEAF, 2 - 3 CLOVES
- ◆ SALT ◆ PEPPER ◆ SUGAR

FOR THE SAUCE
- ◆ 4 TABLESPOONS FLOUR
- ◆ 4 TABLESPOONS OLIVE OIL
- ◆ 2 TEACUPS MILK
- ◆ 2 EGGS
- ◆ 1 TEACUP GRATED CHEESE
- ◆ SALT ◆ PEPPER ◆ NUTMEG

Slice a piece from the top of each tomato and remove the inside.

Heat the oil in a saucepan and fry the onions until golden brown. Add the minced meat, the bay leaf and the inside of the tomatoes. Season with salt and pepper. Stir for some minutes. Add the wine and cook over a moderate heat for 40 minutes. Turn the heat off and add some grated cheese. Sprinkle the inside of the tomatoes with sugar and stuff them with the mixture. Prepare the sauce and pour over each tomato.

Sprinkle with the rest of the cheese. Add a glass of water and bake in a hot oven for 20-25 minutes. Serve hot.

* The sauce is the same with the one used for stuffed artichokes. It becomes more or less thick depending on how much milk is used.

FOR 4 PERSONS

Thessaly

KAPAMAS   **

MEATBALLS WITH EGG AND LEMON SAUCE

- ◆ 500 gr. MINCED MEAT (BEEF OR VEAL)
- ◆ 1 MEDIUM SIZED ONION FINELY CHOPPED
- ◆ 3 EGGS
- ◆ 1/2 - 1 TEACUP PARSLEY FINELY CHOPPED
- ◆ OREGANO
- ◆ 1 SLICE OF BREAD
- ◆ 2 TABLESPOONS FLOUR
- ◆ 230 gr. OLIVE OIL
- ◆ 1 LEMON (JUICE)
- ◆ SALT ◆ PEPPER
- ◆ FRYING OIL
- ◆ 1 litre HOT WATER

Mix the minced meat with the slice of bread (after soaking it in water), one egg, the onion, some oregano, the parsley. Season with salt and pepper. Shape into meatballs and fry slightly.

Heat 180 gr. olive oil in a saucepan and brown the flour. Add 1/2 litre hot water. Stir well with a wooden ladden until it is brought into boiling point. Add the meatballs and cook for 45 minutes.

Heat 50 gr. olive oil, add some pepper and pour over the meatballs. Beat the two eggs, adding the lemon juice slowly and pour over the meatballs.

Serve hot.

FOR 6 PERSONS

ARTICHOKES WITH MINCED MEAT AND CREAM (top)
STUFFED TOMATOES (left)
BAKED AUBERGINES WITH MINCED MEAT AND CREAM (right)

POULTRY AND GAME

* EASY PREPARATION
**MEDIUM DIFFICULTY ***COMPLEX PREPARATION

Lesvos

KOTOPOULO GEMISTO   **

STUFFED CHICKEN

- ◆ 1 CHICKEN WITH THE ENTRAILS
- ◆ 1 GARLiC ◆ 6 LEMONS (JUICE)
- ◆ 50 gr. OLIVES PEELED
- ◆ 4 SLICES HARD CHEESE
- ◆ 1/2 TEACUP OLIVE OIL
- ◆ 1/2 TEACUP COARSELY CHOPPED RUSK
- ◆ OREGANO ◆ CINNAMON ◆ CLOVE
- ◆ SALT ◆ PEPPER

Wash and rub the chicken with lemon and salt. Leave it for 1/2 hour.

Chop the entrails finely, sprinkle with the spice. Heat half the oil in a saucepan and fry the entrails until golden brown. Pour over some of the lemon juice and turn the heat off. Add two tablespoons of the rusk and the olives.

Stuff the chicken with the mixture adding the cheese as well and sew the opening. Rub the chicken with oil and sprinkle with the rest of the lemon juice. Bake in a pre - heated oven at 250° C for almost 1 hour. Remove the liquid from the baking pan every now and then to keep the chicken dry. This liquid can be used to make sauce.

FOR 6 PERSONS

Attica

KOTOPOULO LADORIGANI   *

CHICKEN WITH OIL AND OREGANO SAUCE

- ◆ 1 CHICKEN WEIGHING 1 kilo
- ◆ 80 gr. OLIVE OIL
- ◆ 3 LEMONS (JUICE)
- ◆ OREGANO ◆ SALT ◆ PEPPER

Cut the chicken in serving pieces, take the skin off and put in a bowl with the lemon juice, the oil. Season with oregano, salt and pepper. Leave for an hour. Bake the pieces on a grill in a moderate oven. Turn the chicken pieces over often and sprinkle with the oil and oregano sauce and the lemon juice.

FOR 4 PERSONS

Epirus

KOTOPOULO ME PIPERIES   **

CHICKEN WITH GREEN PEPPERS

- ◆ 1 CHICKEN WEIGHING 1 kilo
- ◆ 4 GREEN PEPPERS CUT IN RINGS
- ◆ 4 ONIONS SLICED
- ◆ 4 TOMATOES SLICED
- ◆ 4 CLOVES OF GARLIC FINELY CHOPPED
- ◆ 2 TABLESPOONS FRESH BASIL
- ◆ 180 gr. OLIVE OIL
- ◆ 1 RED PEPPER
- ◆ CINNAMON ◆ CLOVE ◆ PIMENTO
- ◆ SALT ◆ PEPPER

Cut the chicken into pieces, wash and strain.

Heat the oil in a saucepan and fry the chicken until golden brown. Add the tomatoes, the peppers and the onions and fry until golden brown. Add the basil, the garlic, the clove and the red pepper. Season with cinnamon, salt, pepper and pimento. Add a glass of water and simmer over a low heat for almost 1 hour.

Add hot water if necessary.

FOR 6 PERSONS

STUFFED CHICKEN (right)
CHICKEN WITH OIL AND OREGANO SAUCE (bottom)
CHICKEN WITH GREEN PEPPERS (top)

Thessaly

KOTOPOULO ME HYLOPITTES **
CHICKEN WITH NOODLES

- ◆ 1 CHICKEN WITH THE ENTRAILS WEIGHING 1.5-2 kilos
- ◆ 180 gr. OLIVE OIL ◆ 500 gr. NOODLES
- ◆ 2 ONIONS FINELY CHOPPED
- ◆ 5 TOMATOES RIPE
- ◆ CINNAMON ◆ CLOVE
- ◆ SALT ◆ PEPPER

Wash the chicken, cut in pieces and chop the entrails finely.
Heat half of the oil in a saucepan and fry the chicken until golden brown. Place it on a plate. Heat the rest of the oil in a different saucepan and fry the onions until golden brown. Add the entrails, the tomatoes (finely chopped and strained) and the chicken. Season with cinnamon, clove, salt and pepper. Add some hot water. Cook over a low heat for 1 hour. When done, add 2 1/2 glasses of hot

water and when they reach the boiling point, add the noodles.
Cook until there is no water left.

FOR 6 PERSONS

Roumeli

LAGOS LEMONATOS **
HARE WITH LEMON SAUCE

- ◆ 1 HARE WEIGHING 1.5 - 2 kilos
- ◆ 10 LEMONS ◆ 5 CLOVES GARLIC
- ◆ 200 gr. OLIVE OIL ◆ 1 GLASS WINE
- ◆ 1/2 kilo FETA CHEESE ◆ SALT ◆ PEPPER

Cut the hare in serving pieces and soak in the juice of three lemons for 12 hours. Heat the oil in a saucepan. Add the garlic and the hare and fry until golden brown. Pour the wine over. Add the rest of the lemon juice. Season with salt and pepper. Cook over a low heat until the meat is tender. Add the feta cheese crumbled with a fork before turning the heat off.

FOR 6 PERSONS

Lesvos

KOTOPOULO ME KARYDIA *
CHICKEN WITH NUTS

- ◆ 1 SMALL CHICKEN
- ◆ 2 CLOVES GARLIC ◆ 2 TOASTS
- ◆ 1 TEACUP NUTS POUNDED
- ◆ SALT ◆ PEPPER

Wash and cook the chicken in salted water over a moderate heat for 45 minutes or until tender. Turn the heat off. Pour the stock in a bowl and soak the toasts in it. Pound the garlic with the nuts, add the toasts strained. Season with salt and pepper. Mix well adding

CHICKEN WITH NUTS (left)   CHICKEN WITH OKRA CASSEROLE (right)

stock slowly.

Cut the chicken in serving pieces and pour the sauce over them.

FOR 4 PERSONS

Peloponnese

KOTOPOULO ME BAMIES   **

CHICKEN WITH OKRA CASSEROLE

◆ 1 BIG CHICKEN
◆ 1 kilo OKRA
◆ 2 ONIONS FINELY CHOPPED
◆ 1/2 TEACUP VINEGAR
◆ 1 kilo FRESH TOMATOES FINELY CHOPPED
◆ 180 gr. OLIVE OIL
◆ SALT ◆ PEPPER

Wash and clean the okra. Place in a baking pan and sprinkle with the vinegar. Season with salt and pepper and leave in the sun for 12 hours.

Cut the chicken into pieces. Season with salt and pepper. Heat half the oil in a saucepan. Fry the onions and the chicken until golden brown. Add the tomatoes. Cook over a low heat for almost 1 hour.

Heat the rest of the oil in a frying pan and fry the okra until golden brown. Put them in the saucepan with the chicken. Add 1/2 glass of hot water.

Cook for 10-15 minutes.

FOR 6 PERSONS

111

Macedonia

KOTOPOULO KALOKERINO ✦✦

CHICKEN CASSEROLE WITH VEGETABLES

- ◆ 1 SMALL CHICKEN
- ◆ 1/2 kilo TOMATOES CHOPPED
- ◆ 500 gr. COURGETTES CHOPPED
- ◆ 3 GREEN PEPPERS CHOPPED
- ◆ 1/2 kilo POTATOES CHOPPED
- ◆ 220 gr. OLIVE OIL
- ◆ 1 ONION FINELY CHOPPED
- ◆ SALT ◆ PEPPER

Cut and clean the chicken. Heat the oil in a saucepan and fry the chicken until golden brown. Add the onion, season with salt and pepper. Cover with water and cook over a low heat for 40 minutes. Add the vegetables.
Cook until there is no water left and the sauce is set.

FOR 6 PERSONS

Crete

KOTOPOULO ME PORTOKALI ✦✦

CHICKEN WITH ORANGE JUICE

- ◆ 1 CHICKEN WEIGHING 1 kilo
- ◆ 3 BIG ORANGES (JUICE)
- ◆ 100 gr. BUTTER
- ◆ 100 gr. OLIVE OIL
- ◆ 1 LEMON (JUICE)
- ◆ 1 ONION FINELY CHOPPED
- ◆ SALT ◆ PEPPER
- ◆ 2 GLASSES HOT WATER

Heat the butter and the oil in a saucepan and fry the chicken on all sides until golden brown. Pour the orange and lemon juice over. Add the onion. Season with salt and pepper. Add two glasses

hot water. Cook over a low heat for 1.5 hour.

FOR 6 PERSONS

Thessaly

KAVROUMAS ✦✦

CHICKEN STEW

- ◆ 1 CHICKEN WEIGHING 1 kilo
- ◆ 2 ONIONS FINELY CHOPPED
- ◆ 2 BAY LEAVES
- ◆ 180 gr. OLIVE OIL
- ◆ 1/2 kilo TOMATOES FINELY CHOPPED
- ◆ SALT ◆ PEPPER
- ◆ SOME FLOUR

Cut the chicken in pieces. Put in a saucepan over a low heat to draw the juices. Add some oil and season with salt and pepper and fry until golden brown. Add two glasses of water and cook over a very low heat until there is only little stock left.
Turn the heat off and put the chicken and the stock in a bowl. Put the rest of the oil and the onions in the saucepan. Put again over heat and fry the onions until golden brown. Season with the spice. Add the chicken with the stock and the tomatoes and cook until there is no water left.

FOR 4 PERSONS

CHICKEN CASSEROLE WITH VEGETABLES (right)
CHICKEN WITH ORANGE JUICE (left)

Peloponnese

PAPIA ME ELIES ✶✶
DUCK WITH OLIVES

- ◆ 1 DUCK WEIGHING 1-1 1/2 kilo
- ◆ 3 TOMATOES FINELY CHOPPED
- ◆ 2 ONIONS
- ◆ 180 gr. OLIVE OIL
- ◆ 300 gr. BIG OLIVES (GREEN or BLACK)
- ◆ 2 BAY LEAVES ◆ CLOVE ◆ CINNAMON
- ◆ 1 GLASS WHITE WINE
- ◆ 1 CLOVE GARLIC
- ◆ ROSEMARY
- ◆ SALT ◆ PEPPER
- ◆ 2 GLASSES HOT WATER

Heat the oil in a saucepan and fry the onions until golden brown. Wash the duck and fry it on all sides in the saucepan until golden brown. Pour the wine over it. Add the tomatoes, the olives and the garlic. Season with the spices.

Add two glasses of hot water. Cook over a moderate heat for 1.5 hour or until there is only the sauce left.

FOR 4-6 PERSONS

Epirus

KOTOPOULO GEMISTO ME RYZI ✶✶
CHICKEN STUFFED WITH RICE

- ◆ 1 BIG CHICKEN
- ◆ 2 TEACUPS RICE
- ◆ 2 ONIONS FINELY CHOPPED
- ◆ 1/2 - 1 TEACUP PARSLEY FINELY CHOPPED
- ◆ 500 gr. FETA CHEESE
- ◆ 150 gr. OLIVE OIL ◆ 100 gr. BUTTER
- ◆ OREGANO
- ◆ SALT ◆ PEPPER

DUCK WITH OLIVES

Wash and clean the chicken.
Cook in salted water over a moderate heat for almost 45 minutes. Heat the oil and the butter in a frying pan and fry

114

the onions until golden brown. Add the rice, the parsley, half the cheese. Season with oregano, salt and pepper. Add 5 teacups of the chicken stock. Stir well. Stuff the chicken with the mixture, add the rest of the cheese. Tie the chicken with string.

Bake until there is no water left and the chicken is golden brown.

FOR 6 PERSONS

Peloponnese

LAGOS STIFADO   **

HARE CASSEROLE WITH ONIONS

- ◆ 1 HARE WEIGHING ABOUT 1 kilo
- ◆ 1 kilo SMALL ONIONS
- ◆ 3 CLOVES GARLIC FINELY CHOPPED
- ◆ 1 kilo TOMATOES FINELY CHOPPED
- ◆ 1/2 WINE GLASS VINEGAR
- ◆ 180 gr. OLIVE OIL
- ◆ 6 BAY LEAVES
- ◆ 6 CLOVES
- ◆ 1 TABLESPOON SUGAR
- ◆ SALT ◆ PEPPER

Cut the hare into pieces. Clean the onions in lukewarm water.
Heat the oil in a saucepan and fry the hare and the onions until golden brown. Add the garlic, the tomatoes, the sugar and the vinegar. Season with the spices. Cover with water. Cook over a moderate heat until there is no water left.

FOR 6 PERSONS

Macedonia

AGRIOGOUROUNO KRASATO   **

WILD BOAR CASSEROLE WITH WINE SAUCE

- ◆ 1.5 kilo WILD BOAR
- ◆ 400 gr. SMALL CORN
- ◆ 2 TOMATOES FINELY CHOPPED
- ◆ 1 RED PEPPER
- ◆ 3 ONIONS FINELY CHOPPED
- ◆ 1 GLASS RED WINE
- ◆ 180 gr. OLIVE OIL
- ◆ SALT ◆ PEPPER
- ◆ ROSEMARY ◆ CINNAMON

Heat the oil in a saucepan. Fry the onions until golden brown. Add the wild boar cut in serving pieces. Mix

well. Pour the wine over. Add the tomatoes, the pepper, the corn. Season with the spices. Cook over a low heat for 1.5 hour adding water if necessary.

FOR 6 PERSONS

Thrace

ORTYKIA ME RYZI   **

QUAILS WITH RICE

- ◆ 12 QUAILS
- ◆ 500 gr. RICE
- ◆ 2 TOMATOES FINELY CHOPPED
- ◆ 2 ONIONS
- ◆ 180 gr. OLIVE OIL
- ◆ 1 CLOVE GARLIC FINELY CHOPPED
- ◆ COARSE PEPPER ◆ CINNAMON ◆ SALT
- ◆ 1 litre HOT WATER

Heat the oil in a saucepan and fry the onions until golden brown. Wash and clean the quails and put them in the saucepan. Fry for 10 minutes. Add the tomatoes and the garlic. Season with the spices. Cover with water and cook over a low heat for almost 1.5 hour. Add 1 litre hot water and when it reaches boiling point, add the rice.
Cook until there is no water left.

FOR 6 PERSONS

QUAILS WITH RICE (left)
HARE CASSEROLE WITH ONIONS (right)
WILD BOAR CASSEROLE WITH WINE SAUCE (top0

VEGETABLES

* EASY PREPARATION
**MEDIUM DIFFICULTY ***COMPLEX PREPARATION

Chios

GEMISTA ★★

STUFFED TOMATOES AND GREEN PEPPERS

- ◆ 6 BIG TOMATOES
- ◆ 6 BIG GREEN PEPPERS
- ◆ 3 POTATOES
- ◆ 500 gr. ONIONS FINELY CHOPPED
- ◆ 1/2 - 1 TEACUP RICE
- ◆ 2 TEACUPS OLIVE OIL
- ◆ 1/2 TEACUP PARSLEY FINELY CHOPPED
- ◆ SALT ◆ PEPPER

Wash the tomatoes and the green peppers and cut a thin slice from the stem end. (These must be kept to be used later). Scoop out the seeds and the pulp. Heat the oil in a saucepan and fry the onions until golden brown. Add the rice, the parsley, the dill and the tomato pulp. Season with salt and pepper. Mix well. Fill the tomatoes and the green peppers with the mixture. Cover with the tops. Cut the potatoes in long slices. Arrange the tomatoes, the green peppers and the potatoes in an oiled baking pan. Bake in a moderate oven for almost 45 minutes.

FOR 6 PERSONS

Macedonia

BRIAMI ★

BAKED POTATOES, COURGETTES, AUBERGINES

- ◆ 1 kilo POTATOES
- ◆ 4 MEDIUM-SIZED COURGETTES
- ◆ 2 AUBERGINES
- ◆ 1/2 kilo TOMATOES
- ◆ 4 ONIONS FINELY CHOPPED
- ◆ 3 GREEN PEPPERS

- ◆ 1/2 TEACUP PARSLEY FINELY CHOPPED
- ◆ 1 TEACUP OIL
- ◆ SALT ◆ PEPPER

Clean and slice the potatoes, the courgettes, the green peppers and the aubergines. Place them in an oiled baking pan. Add the onions, the tomatoes sliced and cleaned, the parsley, the oil, salt and pepper. Bake in a moderate oven for almost an hour.

FOR 6-8 PERSONS

Attica

SPANAKORYZO ★

SPINACH WITH RICE

- ◆ 1 kilo SPINACH
- ◆ 1 TEACUP RICE
- ◆ 1 ONION FINELY CHOPPED
- ◆ 1/2 TEACUP DILL
- ◆ 1 TEACUP OLIVE OIL
- ◆ 2 LEMONS (JUICE)
- ◆ 3 GLASSES HOT WATER
- ◆ SALT ◆ PEPPER

Heat the oil in a saucepan and fry the onions until golden brown. Add the dill, the spinach and the three glasses of water. When in boiling point, add the rice, salt and pepper. Cook over a low heat until there is no water left. Pour lemon juice over it to serve.

FOR 6 PERSONS

STUFFED TOMATOES AND GREEN PEPPERS (bottom)
BAKED POTATOES, COURGETTES, AUBERGINES (top)
SPINACH WITH RICE (right)

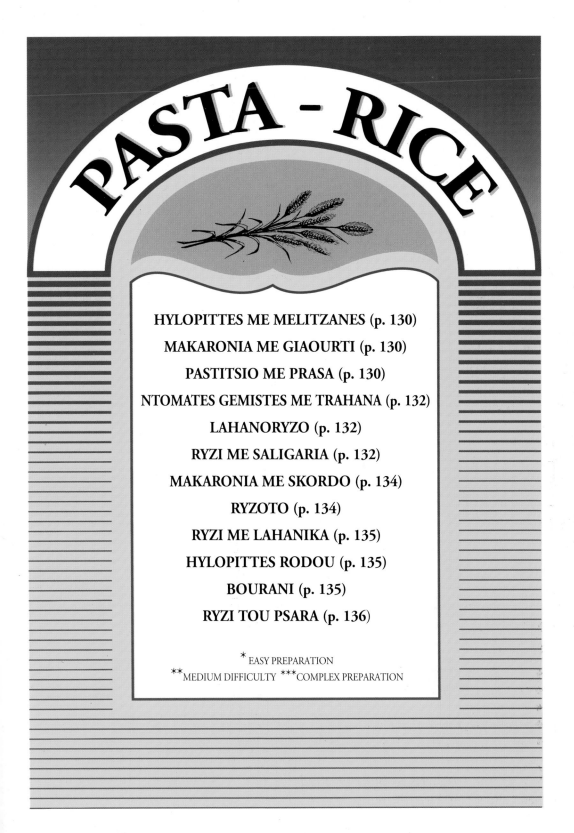

PASTA - RICE

*EASY PREPARATION
**MEDIUM DIFFICULTY ***COMPLEX PREPARATION

A COUPLE OF THRESHERS IN MACEDONIA

Macedonia

CHYLOPITTES ME MELITZANES *
SQUARE NOODLES WITH AUBERGINES

- ◆ 1/2 kilo SQUARE NOODLES
- ◆ 1/2 kilo FRESH TOMATOES
- ◆ 1 kilo AUBERGINES
- ◆ 120 gr. OLIVE OIL
- ◆ 3 TABLESPOONS BUTTER
- ◆ 2 CLOVES GARLIC FINELY CHOPPED
- ◆ 1 TEACUP GRATED CHEESE
- ◆ SALT ◆ PEPPER

Clean and wash the aubergines. Cut them in two. Season with salt and leave them for an hour.

Peel the tomatoes and mash well.

Put the oil, the garlic, the tomato puree in a saucepan. Season with salt and pepper. Cook for 10 minutes. Slice the aubergines and put them in the saucepan. Simmer for 40 minutes.

Cook the square noodles in boiling salted water. Strain. Stir in the butter until it melts.

Sprinkle with the cheese, pour the sauce over them and serve.

FOR 6 PERSONS

Dodecannese

MACARONIA ME GIAOURTI *
SPAGHETTI WITH YOGHOURT

- ◆ 1/2 kilo SPAGHETTI
- ◆ 1/2 kilo STRAINED YOGHOURT
- ◆ 2 ONIONS
- ◆ 3 TABLESPOONS BUTTER
- ◆ SALT

Cook the spaghetti in boiling salted water and strain. Heat the butter and the onions in a frying pan until golden brown. Stir in the yoghourt blending thoroughly. Place the spaghetti on a plate. Pour the sauce over and serve.

FOR 4 PERSONS

Macedonia

PASTITSIO ME PRASA **
SPAGHETTI WITH LEEKS

- ◆ 1/2 kilo SPAGHETTI No 5
- ◆ 1/2 kilo LEEKS
- ◆ 1 TEACUP FRESH BUTTER
- ◆ 1.5 kilo RIPE TOMATOES CUT IN RINGS
- ◆ 1 RED PEPPER
- ◆ 3 EGGS
- ◆ SALT ◆ PEPPER

Half-cook the spaghetti in boiling salted water. Strain and mix with half the butter. Place them on the bottom of a buttered pan. Clean and wash the leeks. Slice them lengthwise (each slice should be 8cm.long) Cook them in salted water,strain and brown in a frying pan with the rest of the butter.

Cover the macaroni with the leeks.

Season with pepper. Cover the leeks with the tomatoes and the red pepper. Bake in a moderate oven for almost 1/2 hour. When the tomatoes are soft, beat the eggs and pour them over. Season with salt and pepper and bake until the surface becomes golden brown.

FOR 6-8 PERSONS

SQUARE NOODLES WITH AUBERGINES (left)
SPAGHETTI WITH YOGHOURT (top)
SPAGHETTI WITH LEEKS (right)

Peloponnese

NTOMATES GEMISTES ME TRACHANA **
TOMATOES STUFFED WITH FRUMENTI

- ◆ 8 BIG RIPE TOMATOES
- ◆ 2 TEACUPS SOUR FRUMENTI
- ◆ 1 TEACUP OLIVE OIL
- ◆ 1 EGG
- ◆ 1 TEACUP MILK
- ◆ 100 gr. FETA CHEESE
- ◆ FRESH MINT
- ◆ SALT ◆ PEPPER
- ◆ 1 ONION FINELY CHOPPED

Slice a piece from the top of each tomato and remove the pulp with a teaspoon. Heat the oil in a saucepan and fry the onion until golden brown. Turn the heat off and add the milk, the frumenti, the egg, the feta cheese crumbled.
Season with fresh mint, salt and pepper. Mix with the pulp from the tomatoes. Stuff each tomato with the mixture and replace the tops. Place them in an oiled baking pan and bake in a moderate oven for 40 minutes.

FOR 4 PERSONS

Epirus

LAHANORYZO *
CABBAGE WITH RICE

- ◆ 250 gr. RICE
- ◆ 1 MEDIUM SIZE CABBAGE COARSELY CHOPPED
- ◆ 1 ONION FINELY CHOPPED
- ◆ 3 TABLESPOONS OLIVE OIL
- ◆ 1/2 - 1 TEACUP PARLSEY FINELY CHOPPED
- ◆ 1/2 kilo TOMATOES
- ◆ SALT, PEPPER
- ◆ 3 TEACUPS HOT WATER

Slice the cabbage. Heat the oil in a saucepan and fry the cabbage with the onion until golden brown. Grate the tomatoes and put them in the saucepan. Cook for 15 minutes. Add the 3 teacups of hot water. When it reaches the boiling point, add the parsley and the rice. Season with salt and pepper. Cook until there is no water left.

FOR 4 PERSONS

Crete

RYZI ME SALIGARIA **
RICE WITH SNAILS

- ◆ 1/2 kilo SNAILS
- ◆ 1 kilo RIPE TOMATOES
- ◆ 1/2 TEACUP RICE
- ◆ 2 CLOVES GARLIC
- ◆ 150 gr. OLIVE OIL
- ◆ 1/2 - 1 TEACUP PARSLEY FINELY CHOPPED
- ◆ CINNAMON ◆ SALT ◆ PEPPER
- ◆ 5 TEACUPS HOT WATER

Boil the snails for 10 minutes, clean them and make a hole in the rear with a fork.
Heat the oil in a saucepan and fry the snails slightly with the garlic and the parsley. Add the tomatoes. Season with salt, pepper and cinnamon. Cook over a low heat for 20 minutes. Add five teacups hot water and when it reaches the boiling point, add the rice. Cook until there is no water left.

FOR 6 PERSONS

TOMATOES STUFFED WITH FRUMENTI (top right)
CABBAGE WITH RICE (left)
RICE WITH SNAILS (right bottom)

Cyclades

MACARONIA ME SKORDO *

SPAGHETTI WITH GARLIC

- ◆ 1/2 kilo SPAGHETTI
- ◆ 3 CLOVES GARLIC FINELY CHOPPED
- ◆ 1/2 - 1 TEACUP PARSLEY FINELY CHOPPED
- ◆ 4 TABLESPOONS OLIVE OIL
- ◆ SALT ◆ PEPPER

Cook the spaghetti in boiling salted water. Heat 3 tablespoons of oil in a small frying pan.Fry the garlic until golden brown.Season with salt. Pour it over the spa-ghetti adding the parsley and a tablespoon oil.Season with pepper.

FOR 4 PERSONS

Attica

RYZOTO *

RICE WITH TOMATOES

- ◆ 1 TEACUP RICE
- ◆ 3 TEACUPS HOT WATER
- ◆ 1/2 TEACUP OLIVE OIL
- ◆ 1/2 kilo FRESH TOMATOES
- ◆ 1/2-1 TEACUP PARSLEY FINELY CHOPPED
- ◆ 2 CLOVES GARLIC FINELY CHOPPED
- ◆ 1 TABLESPOON SUGAR◆ SALT ◆ PEPPER

Peel the tomatoes, remove the seeds and chop finely.
Heat the oil in a saucepan and fry the garlic until golden brown. Add the tomatoes, the parsley, the sugar. Season with salt and pepper. Add 1/2 teacup

water. Cook over a moderate heat for 10 minutes. Add the 3 teacups of hot water. When they reach boiling point, add the rice, stir well and cook until there is no water left.

FOR 4 PERSONS

Crete

RYZI ME LAHANIKA   *
RICE WITH VEGETABLES

- ◆ 300 gr. RICE
- ◆ 100 gr. FRESH BUTTER
- ◆ 300 gr. DIFFERENT VEGETABLES (CARROTS, BEANS, COURGETTES, PEAS, CORN)
- ◆ 1 LEMON (JUICE)
- ◆ SALT ◆ PEPPER

Cook the rice with the lemon juice in boiling water for 15 minutes. Heat the butter in a saucepan and fry the vegetables slightly. Season with salt and pepper. Mix the rice with the vegetables and put them in a cake tin. Turn it over a plate, leave for 5 minutes, remove the cake tin and serve.

FOR 4 PERSONS

Dodecannese

HYLOPITTES RODOU   ***
SQUARE NOODLES FROM RHODES

- ◆ 1 kilo FLOUR
- ◆ 3 EGGS
- ◆ 1 kilo TOMATOES MASHED
- ◆ 1/2 TEACUP FRESH BUTTER
- ◆ SALT
- ◆ 1 TEACUP MILK

Mix the flour with the eggs and the milk and season with salt to prepare dough. Roll out pieces of dough. When dried, roll over a thin stick. Cut in small squares, 1 cm. Let them dry.
Put the tomatoes mashed, the butter and 3 tablespoons water in a saucepan. Season with salt. Cook until boiling point. Add the square noodles and cook over a moderate heat until all the liquid is absorbed.

FOR 8 PERSONS   *Photograph page 136*

Volos

BOURANI   *
RICE WITH GARLIC

- ◆ 2 TEACUPS RICE
- ◆ 1 RED PEPPER SLICED
- ◆ 15 gr. OLIVE OIL
- ◆ 1 ONION
- ◆ 3 CLOVES GARLIC
- ◆ 1/2-1 TEACUP PARSLEY FINELY CHOPPED
- ◆ 1/2 kilo TOMATOES
- ◆ SALT ◆ PEPPER
- ◆ 6 TEACUPS HOT WATER

Heat the oil in a saucepan and fry the onion and the garlic until golden brown. Add the rice and the parsley and stir well. Add the pepper. Grate the tomatoes and add the pulp in the saucepan. Pour over 6 teacups hot water. Cook until there is no water left.

FOR 6 PERSONS   *Photograph page 136*

Dodecannese

RYZI TOY PSARA ✶✶

RICE WITH SEA - FOOD

- ◆ 600 gr. RICE
- ◆ 400 gr. SHRIMPS
- ◆ 200 gr. CRAYFISH
- ◆ 200 gr. MUSSELS
- ◆ 2 ONIONS
- ◆ 1 PEPPER
- ◆ 1 LEMON (JUICE)
- ◆ 2 TABLESPOONS OUZO
- ◆ 1 TEACUP OIL

Heat the oil in a saucepan and fry the onions and the pepper slightly. Add the shrimps, the mussels (after washing them thoroughly) and the crayfish. Cook over a moderate heat for 5 minutes. Pour the ouzo over them. Add the appropriate quantity of hot water (1 teacup rice - 2 teacups water) and then the rice with the lemon juice. Cook for 15 minutes. Serve hot.

FOR 4 PERSONS

SQUARE NOODLES FROM RHODES (left)   RICE WITH GARLIC (right)

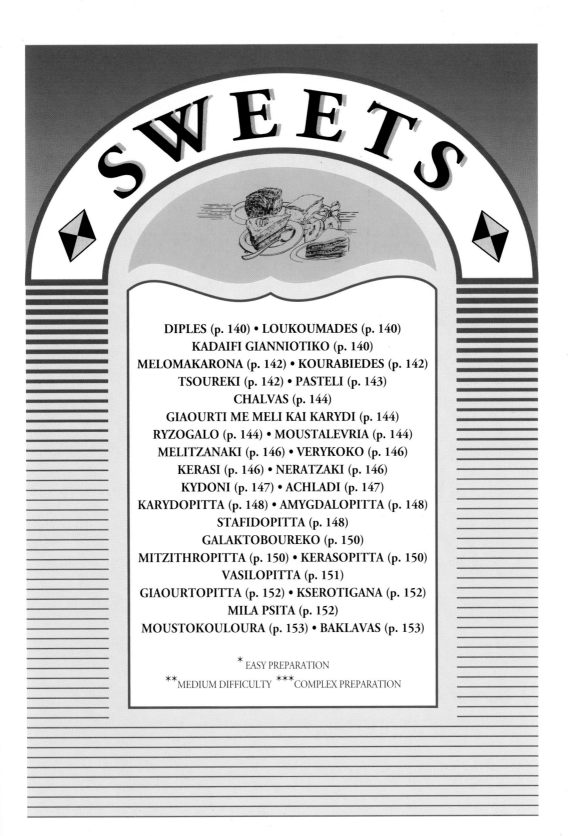

SWEETS

* EASY PREPARATION
**MEDIUM DIFFICULTY ***COMPLEX PREPARATION

Peloponnese

DIPLES ***
SWEET FRIED BOW - KNOTS

For the dough
◆ 10 EGGS
◆ 1/2 TEACUP BRANDY
◆ GRATED RIND OF 3 ORANGES
◆ 1 kilo FLOUR ◆ FRYING OIL
For the syrup
◆ 4 TEACUPS HONEY ◆ 2 TEACUPS SUGAR
◆ 2 TEACUPS WATER
◆ GROUND NUTS ◆ CINNAMON

Beat the eggs with the brandy. Add the grated orange rind and the flour and knead well.

Divide the dough into balls and leave in a warm place for 1 hour. Roll out into thin sheets. Cut into long strips about 5X10 cm. Heat the oil in a saucepan and fry each one separately until golden brown. Put them on a plate.Boil the water, the honey and the sugar until the syrup is set. Pour the syrup in a bowl. Dip the bow knots in the bowl for a minute. Sprinkle with cinnamon and walnuts.

Crete

LOUKOUMADES **
HONEY PUFFS

◆ 500 gr. FLOUR SIEVED, 15 gr. YEAST
◆ 2 GLASSES WATER LUKEWARM
◆ 700 gr. FRYING OIL
◆ 1 TEACUP HONEY, CINNAMON
◆ 1/2 DESSERTSPOON SALT

Dissolve the yeast in a bowl with some water. Add the rest of the water, one tablespoon honey, the salt and the flour.

Mix well and leave it in a warm place for 1 hour.

Heat the oil in a deep frying pan. Drop in the mixture in small spoonfuls and fry. When ready, pour honey over them, sprinkle with cinnamon and serve.

Epirus

KADAIFI GIANNIOTIKO ***
NUT FILLED KADAIFI FROM GIANNENA

◆ 2 EGGS
◆ 1 kilo KADAIFI PASTRY
◆ 300 gr. NUTS POUNDED
◆ 300 gr. MILK BUTTER
◆ 2 TABLESPOONS SUGAR
◆ 4 TABLESPOONS RUSK CRUMBS
For the syrup
◆ 800 gr. SUGAR ◆ 3 TEACUPS WATER
◆ 2 DESSERTSPOONS LEMON JUICE

Beat the egg yolks with the sugar in a bowl until the sugar is dissolved. Add the nuts slowly, the rusk crumbs and finally the whites of the eggs beaten seperately. Whisk the mixture well, add a tablespoon of butter and whisk again.

Divide the kadaifi pastry into serving portions and place a tablespoon filling on each one. Fold well. Place them in a buttered baking pan, 25X40 cm., melt the butter and put one tablespoon over each seperate piece. Bake in a hot oven for 40 minutes.

Boil the water with the sugar. Add the lemon juice towards the end. Continue boiling until the syrup is not too watery. Take the kadaifi out of the oven and pour the syrup over it.

SWEET FRIED BOW - KNOTS (bottom right)
NUT FILLED KADAIFI FROM GIANNENA (top right)
HONEY PUFFS (bottom left) ,PANCAKES FROM CRETE (top left)

Peloponnese

MELITZANAKI ✴✴
AUBERGINE PRESERVE (SPOON SWEET)

- ◆ 500 gr. TINY AUBERGINES UNRIPE
- ◆ 500 gr. SUGAR
- ◆ 1 VANILLA
- ◆ 20 BLANCHED ALMONDS
- ◆ 1 LEMON (JUICE)

Clean the aubergines and leave them in a bowl with water for 5 hours.

Cook them for 5 minutes and then put them in a bowl with water and the lemon juice for 2 hours. Rinse them. Place an almond in each aubergine. Put two glasses of water and the sugar in a saucepan and boil until it sets. Add the aubergines and simmer until the syrup and the aubergines are set. Add the vanilla.

Epirus

VERIKOKO ✴✴
APRICOT PRESERVE (SPOON SWEET)

- ◆ 1 kilo GREEN APRICOTS
- ◆ 1 kilo SUGAR
- ◆ 1 TABLESPOON LEMON JUICE

Wash the apricots and remove the stone without opening them.

Put them in a bowl with water for two hours. Put them in a saucepan with a glass of water, the lemon juice and the sugar and cook until the syrup is set.

Macedonia

KERASI ✴✴
CHERRY PRESERVE (SPOON SWEET)

- ◆ 1 kilo WHITE HEART CHERRIES
- ◆ 1 kilo SUGAR
- ◆ 1 TABLESPOON LEMON JUICE
- ◆ 1 VANILLA

Remove the stones from the cherries without opening them.

Put the sugar with a glass of water in a saucepan and simmer until the syrup sets. Add the cherries and boil until the preserve is set. Remove scum if necessary. Add the lemon juice and the vanilla before turning the heat off.

Chios

NERATZAKI ✴✴
BITTER ORANGE PRESERVE (SPOON SWEET)

- ◆ 25 SMALL GREEN BITTER ORANGES
- ◆ 700 gr. SUGAR

Put them in a saucepan with plenty of water and cook for an hour until they are soft. Rinse them.

With a special knife make a small hole from one end to the other to remove the seeds. Rinse again thoroughly. Leave in a bowl with water for 5 days. Change the water twice a day to remove bitterness.

Put two glasses of water and the sugar in a saucepan and boil until the syrup is set. Remove from heat. Add the bitter oranges and leave them for a day. Boil again until the syrup and the bitter oranges are set.

VARIETY OF DIFFERENT SPOON SWEETS

Sterea

KYDONI ✱✱

QUINCE PRESERVE (SPOON SWEET)

◆ 8 QUINCES
◆ 2 GLASS WATER
◆ 2 GLASS SUGAR
◆ 1 TEACUP BLANCHED ALMONDS

Peel the quinces and grate them coarsely.
Put the sugar with the water in a saucepan and boil to set. Put the quinces in another saucepan with plenty of water and cook for 10 minutes. Strain and put them in the saucepan with the syrup. Add the almonds. Cook for 10 minutes.

Thessaly

ACHLADI ✱✱

PEAR PRESERVE (SPOON SWEET)

◆ 1 kilo SMALL PEARS
◆ 1 kilo SUGAR
◆ 2 LEMONS (JUICE)
◆ 2 VANILLAS

Peel the pears and remove the seeds with a special knife. Put them in a bowl with water and the lemon juice for three hours. Strain them.
Put in a saucepan with a glass of water and the sugar and cook until the syrup is set. Add the vanillas before turning the heat off.

Peloponnese

KARYDOPITTA ✱✱
WALNUT PIE

- ◆ 2 TEACUPS SUGAR, 3 TEACUPS FLOUR
- ◆ 6 EGGS
- ◆ 1 TEACUP SEMOLINA (FINE)
- ◆ 2 TEACUPS OIL
- ◆ 2 TEACUPS GROUND WALNUTS
- ◆ 2 DESSERTSPOONS BAKING SODA
- ◆ 2 DESSERTSPOONS BAKING POWDER
- ◆ 2 DESSERTSPOONS GROUND
  CINNAMON AND CLOVE
- ◆ 1/2 TEACUP BRANDY ◆ 1 TEACUP MILK
  For the syrup
- ◆ 4 TABLESPOONS SUGAR
- ◆ 1 TEACUP HONEY ◆ 3 GLASSES WATER

Beat the egg yolks with the sugar very well. Beat the whites of the eggs separately.

Dissolve the baking soda in the brandy. Put the oil, the semolina, the baking powder, the flour, the soda with the brandy, the milk, the nuts, the cinnamon with the clove and the eggs (yolks and whites) in a bowl and mix well.

Put the mixture in a buttered baking pan, 25X40. Bake in a pre-heated oven at 200 C for 40 minutes.

Boil the water with the honey and the sugar until the syrup sets. Pour it over the pie when it is ready.

Crete

AMYGDALOPITTA ✱✱
ALMOND PIE

- ◆ 700 gr. SUGAR
- ◆ 700 gr. FLOUR
- ◆ 1 GLASS MILK
- ◆ 8 EGGS ◆ 300 gr. BUTTER

- ◆ 1 TEACUP ALMONDS FINELY CHOPPED
- ◆ 1 TABLESPOON BAKING SODA
- ◆ 1 TABLESPOON BAKING POWDER

Beat the butter with the sugar until it becomes white. Add the egg yolks and continue beating.

Dissolve the baking soda in the milk. Pour it over the mixture and add the flour with the baking powder and the almonds. Beat the whites of the eggs separately. Pour them over the mixture. Mix well and place in a buttered baking pan. Bake in a moderate oven for 45 minutes.

Macedonia

STAFIDOPITTA ✱✱
PIE WITH RAISINS

- ◆ 800 gr. SELF RISING FLOUR
- ◆ 1/2 DESSERTSPOON SALT
- ◆ 200 gr. BUTTER ◆ 2 EGGS
- ◆ 1 TEACUP SUGAR
- ◆ 2 TEACUPS RAISINS
- ◆ GRATED ORANGE RIND
- ◆ 300 gr. MILK
- ◆ 50 gr. CONFECTIONERS' SUGAR

Sieve the flour with the salt. Melt the butter and beat it in a bowl. Add the sugar and the eggs beating continuously. Add the raisins, the grated orange rind, the flour and the milk. Mix well and place in a buttered baking pan.

Bake at 200° C for an hour. Sprinkle with the confectioners' sugar when rea-dy.

WALNUT PIE (bottom right)
ALMOND PIE (bottom left) PIE WITH RAISINS (top left)
PIE WITH YOGHOURT (top right)

Attica

GALAKTOBOUREKO ***

MILK PIE

- ◆ 1/2 kilo THIN PASTRY SHEETS READY - MADE
- ◆ 1/2 kilo MILK ◆ 6 EGGS
- ◆ 1 kilo SUGAR
- ◆ 200 gr. SEMOLINA ◆ 1 VANILLA
- ◆ 250 gr. FRESH BUTTER
- ◆ LEMON JUICE

Beat the eggs with half the sugar. Add the semolina beating continuously. Stir in the milk. Continue the stirring over a low heat. When it reaches the boiling point, turn the heat off and add the vanilla. Cover the saucepan.

Put half the pastry sheets in a buttered baking pan (No 34) brushing each one with butter. The edges of the pastry sheets should come up above the top of the pan. Spread the mixture evenly over pastry sheets. Fold the edges over it and cover with the rest of the pastry sheets. Cut in the top pastry sheets with a knife in squares. Pour the rest of the butter over it and spirnkle with water. Bake in a pre-heated oven at 180° C for an hour.

Put the rest of the sugar in a saucepan together with a glass of water and some lemon juice. Cook for 10 minutes until the syrup is set. Pour it over the milk pie when it is cold.

Epirus

MYZITHROPITTA **

CREAM - CHEESE PIE

For the dough
- ◆ 1 1/2 kilo FLOUR
- ◆ 1/2 DESSERTSPOON SALT
- ◆ 1/2 DESSERTSPOON BAKING POWDER
- ◆ 1/2 TEACUP BUTTER
- ◆ 1/4 TEACUP WATER

For the filling
- ◆ 600 gr. CREAM CHEESE UNSALTED
- ◆ 2 EGGS
- ◆ 1/2 TEACUP SUGAR

Prepare the dough mixing the flour, the salt, the baking powder, the butter and the water. Knead well. Put the dough in the fridge for 10-15 minutes. Roll it out in a baking pan. Crumble the cream cheese and mix with the sugar and the eggs. Mix well. Spread the mixture on the dough. Roll the edges over. Bake in a moderate oven for 45 minutes. Pour morello syrup over it and garnish with whipped cream (optional).

Attica

KERASOPITTA **

CHERRY PIE

- ◆ 2 TEACUPS FLOUR
- ◆ 1 DESSERTSPOON BAKING POWDER
- ◆ 1/2 TEACUP BUTTER
- ◆ 1/4 TEACUP WATER
- ◆ 1 kilo CHERRIES
- ◆ 1/2 TEACUP SUGAR
- ◆ 1 TABLESPOON BRANDY
- ◆ 1 TABLESPOON VANILLA

To make the dough: Mix the flour, the baking powder and the butter. Knead adding water. Put it in the fridge for some time. Roll it out in a baking pan (keep some for the end).

Remove the stones from the cherries and mix them with the sugar, the vanilla, the brandy. Place the cherries on the dough.

wine drinking was the main part of the feast. During the feast the guests drank wine and talked at length on a topic which had been priorly agreed upon by all the guests.

It is not by chance that Plato conducted his philosophical dialogues on love during a feast. The wines produced on the islands were considered to be the best during antiquity and in fact, the wines of Chios, Lesvos and Thassos were the most expensive. Seals on the surface of the locally made clay amphorae ensured the authenticity of the wine, many of which have been found in Macedonia, Pontos, Egypt, Sicily and on sites in central Asia such as Kamboul. The discovery of these seals is evidence of the far reaching and extensive commercial trade of Aegean wine.

Wine is a deep rooted tradition in contemporary Greek society which has a history of thousands of years. Testimony of this is the fact that geographically in all areas of Greece one can find a great number of vineyards. The ideal climate and the variety of Greek vineyard soil ensure for the followers of Bacchus a much envied place among the countries which produce wine.

The quantity of wine produced is approximately 500.000.000 litres a year and the processing of grapes occures at 360 wineries which have fermenting facilities amounting to approximately 750,000 cubic meters. The ratio of white to red is 6/4. 10% of the wine produced is V.Q.P.R.D. and the rest are Table Wines which are also commercially successful in barrel (not bottled) form. Greece has patented the age indicator as "Cava" for table wines. The minimum ageing time is two years for white wines and three years for red wines. Many wines sold as barrel wine are on par to V.Q.P.R.D. wines and in many cases superior in terms of aroma and taste since they are usually bought near the location of production. Let us begin our explorations of Greek wines.

RED ON BLACK ATTICAN CRATER DEPICTING A FEAST
4th CENTURY B.C., ATHENS, ARCHAEOLOGICAL MUSEUM

Peloponnese

The Peloponnese is the largest producing area of wines with geographical locations which grow and produce a series of high quality wines. The main wine producing areas are:

1.NEMEA: The vineyards of Corinth are considered to be, due to the geological formation and climatic conditions, the best in the world. The vineyards stretch across an area which begins along the shore of the sea and reaches up along slopes of 800m altitude, often embracing ancient temples. In this expanse the smaller area of Nemea is deemed to yield a variety of high quality

Greek vines, among which is the **Agiorgitiko**, a strand that is not cultivated anywhere else. From this variety of grapes, the superior quality **NEMEA** wines are produced. Due to its deep red colouring this wine is also known as "the blood of Hercules". It's an almost black in colour wine and rich in body. It is fermented in oak barrels and has a distinctly aromatic bouquet.

2.MANTINIA: The **Moschophilero** grapes, of exceedingly fine quality, are cultivated here in the heart of the Peloponnese at an altitude of 650m to produce a dry white wine with a slightly high acidity count, a delicate aroma and a distinct fruit flavour.

3.PATRA: In the towns located southeast of Patra the vineyards which yield the **Mavrodaphni** grapes incline upwards along the mountain slopes. A sweet wine is produced from a combination of these grapes and **black Corinthian** grapes, which has to ferment in oak barrels for many years in order to aquire the qualities inherent in the **Mavrodaphni Patron** wine. Another strand of grapes called **Moschato** white is also cultivated in this area. From these grapes a series of sweet wines is produced whose colourings are light topaz and which exhude a wonderful aroma. These wines are known by the names **Moschatos Patron and Moschatos Rio Patron.** Along the slopes of the Panachaikou mountain range, 200 and 450 meters away from the sea, the **Roditis** grape is cultivated, which completes the feast of grapes grown in the area. The grape is named after its rose colouring and the wine which is produced from these grapes can be found on the market with its distinct trade name Patra which is indicative of its high quality. Other smaller vineyards can be found throughout the Peloponnese which produce their own wines, less known but of excellent quality nonetheless and worthy of your attention.

Crete

The most traditional European vinery region harbouring a host of grape strands which are protected by the warm African currents and which yield a series of wines of exceptional quality.

1.SITIA AND DAPHNES: The **Liatiko** grape is cultivated in great abundance on the eastern shore of the island in the region of Sitia and is one of the oldest types grown in the Mediterranean. *Sitia wine* is a characteristically Mediterranean dry red wine. In the area of Heracleion, a sweet wine named **Malzavias** is produced from the same grapes. The **Liatiko** grape is also found in the area of Daphnes, which also produces the red wine **Daphnes** identical in type to the Sitia wine.

2.ARCHANES AND PEZA: From the **Kotsiphali** grape and the dark coloured **Manthilaria** grape the red wines **Archanes** and **Peza** are produced. The area of Peza produces rose and red table wines from the extensive vineyards where a variety of grapes such as **Soulvania, Rozaki, Vilana, Kotsiphali and Manthilaria** are cultivated. A mixture of the last two produces a red dry wine named **Peza (Mantiko)** while the **Vilana** grapes yield the dry white wine named Peza.

Central Greece and Euboea

The wine producing areas of Attica, Boetia and Euboea essentially compose one entity.

DANCING COUPLE IN THE MIDST OF DIONYSIAN ECSTASY,IVORY,DISCOVERED IN THE ROYAL TOMBS OF VERGINA,4th CENTURY ARCHAEOLOGICAL MUSEUM OF SALONICA

This is primarily due to the white grapes strand known as **Savatiano,** which is cultivated in this vast area. The famous *retsina* is only one type of wine produced from this grape strand. The slight variations in climatic conditions throughout the area contribute to the differences in the characteristics of the wines even though they are produced from the same grape strand. A dry white wine commercially known as *Kanza Attica* is produced in this region while all the other wines produced here are table wines.

Macedonia and Thrace

From ancient times the areas of Macedonia and Thrace were reknown for their superior quality wines. The present area of cultivated vineyards is smaller than in previous periods due to the sudden attack of vine lice 70 years ago.

1.NAOUSSA-AMYNTAIO-GOUMENISSA:
The vineyards of Naoussa are located along the slopes of the Vermio mountain range at an altitude of 350m. It is here that the most famous grape strand in Northern Greece is cultivated the **Xinomavro**. *Naoussa* is a dark coloured wine with a rich body. It must be extensively aged for it to aquire its mildness and aroma. The same strand is also cultivated in *Amyntaio* but due to the different altitude height of this area, the wine which is produced here acquires different characteristics. In Goumenissa the Xiromavro is cultivated together with another strand called **Negoska**. These two strands produce an exceptionally savoury wine named *Goumenissa.*

2.PLAGIES MELITONA In the large privately owned vineyards of Chalkidiki, the French Greek bond of friendship performs miracles. There,the oldest Greek strand, **Limnia**, is cultivated together with the French **Cabernet Sauvignion and Cabernet Franc**, to produce an exquisitely dry red wine. The refreshingly tasting white wine of the area is produced from a mixture of **Roditis, Athiri and Asirtiko** grapes.These strands and other strand variations are cultivated at the monasteries of Agion Oros whose facilities produce white and red wines commercially known as *Topikos Agioritikos Inos*.

Ionian Islands

Zakynthos, Lefkada and Corfu almost exclusively produce table wines, the most well known being the *Verdea* wine.
Kefalonia produces two exceptional sweet wines known as

BARRELS IN TAVERN

Moschatos Kefallinias and Mavrodaphni Kefallinias while along the semi mountainous region of the island the famous **Robola** strand is cultivated, an exceptional white grape which produces the bottled wine *Robola Kefallinias*. A red variety known as Vertzani is found on the island of Lefkada.

Epirus

Even though this region is not among the main vinery regions of Greece it is, nonetheless, known for its two wines: **Zitsa** and **Metsovo**. Zitsa is produced from the local grapes **Debina**, cultivated in the areas northwest of Ioannina in the village of Zitsa which has two types of wines: A light dry white wine which has a fruity flavour and a natural bubbly wine which is bottled dry or semi sweet.

The French strand **Cabernet Sauvignion** has found ideal cultivating conditions in the area of Metsovo where it produces a wonderful red wine, rich in body and aged in oak barrels.

Thessaly

There are four distinct vineyard regions in Thessaly. Tirnavos which yeilds the **Moschaton Hamburg** grapes only for eating.
Karditsa cultivates **Mavro Mesenikola** for its red wine and **Batiki** for its white.
Three grape strands are grown in the area of Neas Aghialou: the red **Sikiotis**, the white **Savatiano** and the **Roditis** whose characteristic colour is pink. From the last two grape strands the wine commercially known as **Aghialou,** a superior quality wine, is produced. Lastly, the vineyard regions of Rapsanis is located in the valley of Tebi, one of the most beautiful areas of Greece. From three strands of grape, **Xinomavro, Krasato** and **Stavroto**, the high

quality red wine commercially known as **Rapsani** is produced.

The Islands of the Eastern Aegean

Samos, Chios, Lesvos and Limnos hold the wine producing regions of the eastern Aegean. Of these, Samos is the most significant followed by Limnos. Chios at one time was reknown for its wine but it is now a mere reflection of its past wine making glory which was destroyed in a fire by the Turks in 1821.

SAMOS: The vineyards of the island incline upwards along the slopes of the two mountains Abelo and Kerki up to an altitude of 800m. The Moschato white is the main grape strand cultivated on the island and even though it is found in other areas, it does not yield the famous nectar that the island strand has. This is due not only to the island ecosystem but also to the different method of wine production. The wine is distributed on the market and is commercially known by the name **Samos.**

LIMNOS: The fame of the island's wines owes it origins to antiquity. The eastern side of the island produces the **Limnia** strand referred to by Aristotle. From this strand, known today as **Limnos**, a traditional type of red wine is produced. Today, the island of Limnos is known for the wines it produces from the grape strand **Moschato Alexandrias** which yields a dry white wine with a light muscrat fragrance and a sweet white one.

Cyclades

The grape is cultivated on almost all the Cycladic islands, the most reknown being the islands of Paros and Thira.

1.PAROS: The island has given its name to a red wine which is produced from two grape strands: the red **Mandilaria** and the white **Monemvasia.** From these two grape strands the wine **Paros** is produced and aged in oak barrels to acquire its distinctive velvety smooth taste.

THIRA: The wines of Santorini are produced in a unique ecosystem which is not found anywhere else in the world. The porous volcanic soil retains moisture which is then secreted during the night, while the "Meltemia" or the Etesian winds, which blow in August and September, don't allow the drops to stay on the vineleaves for very long. The local strand of the island is considered to be the most eclectic strand in all the Mediterranean. This is the **Asyrtiko** from which a number of outstanding wines is produced.

Dodekannese

Of all these beautiful islands, only Rhodes remains true to the production of wine. The white **Athiri** and the red **Mandilaria** grapes are responsible for the production of two very fine wines: the white wine **Rodos** and the red wine Rodos.

Moschatos Rodos is produced in smaller quantities from the grapes **Moschato white** and **Moschato Trani.**

FOUR DRACHMAS 500 - 480 B.C.

GLOSSARY

Ameletita: Lamb's fries. The testicles of lambs or goats which when prepared make a wonderful appetizer.

Avgolemono: Tasty egg and lemon sauce always beaten by hand and easy to make It is added into soups and other dishes.

Avgotaraho: A wonderful delicacy and very expensive appetizer. The roe of lake fish from the lagoon of Messolonghi and which requires some degree of preparation.

Bougatsa: A type of sweet which looks like a cheese pie but whose filling consists of a sweet cream.

Cafes Ellinikos: Greek coffee is made over a low fire in a small coffee pot and served in a small cup accompanied by a glass of water. The ratio of sugar and coffee is determined by the person who will drink the coffee hence the different names associated with it such as Metrios: equal amount of sugar and coffee; Glykos: more sugar than coffee; and Sketos: no sugar at all. When the coffee is poured into the cup from a fair height to produce bubbles on the surface of the coffee froth then the coffee is called Vrastos. If there are no bubbles on the surface of the coffee froth, that is the coffee has been poured into the cup from the height of the brim, then it is called Varis.

Eleolado: Olive oil is the product of crushed olives. During antiquity the oil was used for lighting as well as for its medicinal properties, but above all it was used extensively for cooking. From antiquity until the present times olive oil has been one of the basic ingredients for cooking and is used in almost all the dishes. The word oil is synonymous to olive oil, all other types of oils are referred to by their proper names. The areas which are re-known for the production of olive oil are Kalamata, Amphissa, Lesvos, Crete and other places.

BASIL

Elia: An ancient bush which was named "Kotinos" domesticated by the ancient Greeks and developed into the sacred olive tree which gives us its fruit, the olive. Today the areas which are touched by the Mediterranean sea yeild this tree in abundance.

Fasolada: The national dish of Greece. Dried beans prepared as a soup and cook-ed with celery, onion and tomato.

Feta: The most popular cheese in Greece and an ancient means of processing sheep's milk. There are three main types: the barrel feta which matures in a wooden barrel; telemes which matures in a metallic container; and the kalathaki which matures in a straw basket. It is never absent from a Greek table and-home and enables the Greeks to hold first place in terms of cheese consumption in Europe. It is an excellent accompaniment to all meals and salads.

Gastra: A cooking utensil which is found predominantly in northern Greece. It is a round metallic utensil which is placed into a large pan over burning embers to produce a wonderful roast.

Giomatari: The fresh barrel wine which comes from a full barrel. This type of wine has a slight opaque clarity.

AVGOTARAHO FROM MESSOLONGHI

Glyko Koutaliou: A sweet preserve which can be found in all kafenia. It boosts your sugar level since it is made of different fruit, flowers or vegetables in a heavy syrup. It is served on a small plate accompanied by a glass of water.

Hasapotaverna: A tavern which has its own butcher's shop on the premises.

Hipovrihio: A type of sweet served in the cafenia and which is a spoonful of a thick white sugary substance whose flavour and aroma may be vanilla or masti-ha and served in a glass of water.

Horta tou Vounou: A variety of wild weeds each with its own name which varies from region to region. The most well known is the rathiki although there are other types whose flavours vary. Raw or boiled, they make wonderful salads.

Kaseri: A type of mild yellow cheese which is produced primarily in central Greece.

Kokkinisto: A means of preparing a number of meat dishes. The meat is first sealed in a mixture of hot oil, finely chopped onion and fresh tomatoes.

Kokoretsi: An ancient dish which is made of sheep entrails passed through a spit and wrapped in intestines which is cooked over burning embers primarily at Easter.

Kondosouvli: Pieces of lamb or pork passed through a spit, seasoned with salt and pepper and roasted..

Koutouki: A small in size tavern. It serves a small selection of dishes and has large barrels filled with abundantly fine retsina which usually is conducive to songs.

Ladera: A large category of dishes which are servedprimarily as main plates. These dishes are almost exclusively of vegetables or cereals cooked in olive oil.

Ladolemono: A mixture of olive oil and fresh lemon juice beaten well and poured over roasts or salads.

Ladorigani: A sauce made of olive oil and dried crushed oregano which is used to paste roasted meat or fish.

Lemonato: A dish (meat dish) which is cooked with a large amount of fresh lemon juice.

Manouri: A fresh cheese which is completely saltless.

Mastiha: A world re-known aromatic product which is produced by the mastiha tree grown only in the mastiha regions on the island of Chios and no-where else. Endeavours to cultivate this tree in other regions have been attempted but without success.

Mitzithra: A cheese which is predominant-ly produced by a fami-ly in their home. The cheese is made of ei-ther lamb or goat milk or a combination of both and can be served fresh or dried and grated.

Ouzo: Vine stems which are distilled and flavoured with anise. Particularly known throughout the world.

Paidakia: Lamb spare ribs cut into small portions and barbaqued over charcoal. This is one of the main roasted dishes, together with lamb cooked on a spit,

MILKING

which are cooked over burning embers in the Greek countryside.

Paksimadia: Rusks made of slices of wheat or rye bread dried in the oven and easy to keep. They are at the same time very tasty especially the rye rusks of Crete and the Cyclades.

Philo: Pastry made of wheat flour and rolled out in thin sheets to be used pri-marily in the preparation of a variety of pittes and pastries.

Pitta: An exculsively Greek dish made of thin pastry filled with cheese, vegetables but also meat. A full course dish which combines the skill of the cook and has the added convenience of being easy to trans-port. The pittas (pies) of Epirus are by far the best.

Retsina: The main barrel wine which is primarily produced in the region of Attica. Its name derives from the retsina or the resin collected from the bark of pine trees and added into the wine to preserve it and to give the wine its distinct aroma.

Riganato: A dish whose main ingredient is oregano.

Rigani: Oregano, a low bush which grows prolifically throughout all Greece and yeilds this herb which is used exten-sively in Greek cooking.

Saganaki: A small frying pan in which appetizers are prepared and served.

Sharas: Whatever is charbroiled on a rack over burning charcoal or embers, primarily meats and fish.

Soropato: Any sweet which has been made in a heavy syrup (sugar dissolved in water).

Sosma: The dregs of barrel wine.

Souvlaki: The most famous fast food meal served throughout Greece. It is made of small cubes of meat or minced meat on a spit and roasted over charcoal. As soon as the meat is ready it is wrapped in a pre-baked pita together with pieces of tomato, onion, parsley and tzaziki.

Souvlas: All meats roasted on a spit.

Spitiko: This describes all food which has been prepared in a home as opposed to food prepared in a restaurant. "Spitiko" characterises and emphasises the food's freshness and superior quality.

Stamnas: Meat which is cooked in a small stamna (clay water pot).

Thimari: A small aromatic bush which grows in barren and dry landscape primarily in the Attica region and on the islands. Its aromatic quality is used in the production of honey and in a great number of other recipes.

Tis Oras: Dishes, mostly meat, which are prepared only when ordered.

Trahanas: A home made pasta produced in many areas of mainland Greece and made of flour, milk and eggs and which is granular.

Tsipouro - Tsikoudia - Raki: Three different names of a drink which is made of distilled vine stems as a rule but figs and mulberries are also used and which is made in the home throughout Greece. Only recently has it been bottled.

Tzaziki: A well known appetizer and which is a mixture of yogurt, garlic and cucumber.

Vasilikos: Basil which is also the symbol of the Greek court. There are two types of this herb, the first has small curly leaves while the second strand has large wide leaves. It is used extensively in cooking both raw and prepared. It also is also a wonderful fly and mosquito repellent.

Xerosphiri: The consumption of wine or ouzo without any accompanying appetizers.

CRETAN WEDDING BREAD